Love &

Courtship

For many couples, love isn't what they thought it would be

Timeless counsel and wisdom by

Bob Garon

First printing: 1992
Second printing: 1993
Third printing: 1995

Published by VGV PUBLICATIONS

Printed in the United States of America.

Cover layout and internal formatting: Francisca de Zwager

For information: P.O Box MCPO 2099, Makati City, Sen Gil Puyat Avenue, Makati City, Philippines, 1260
or www.facebook.com/bobgaron

ISBN: 978-1-7378277-0-2

Royalties earned from this book will help poor children in the Philippines get an education.

This book is dedicated to my lovely wife, Emmy, and to my two wonderful daughters, Vanessa Anne and Maria Alexandra, who have been my source of inspiration.

Contents

Foreword

One of the images I have of my father that will always be a beautiful memory, is of him writing at a desk, with his long yellow pad. He had a constant supply of those writing pads that were always with him everywhere he went. Whether we were on vacation in another country or at home, his writings fueled him. His teachings have inspired many throughout the years.

As a child, one of the most common question my father would randomly ask my sister and I was, "how do you feel?" Early on, we were taught the importance of expressing one's feelings and openly talking about them. We got tired of answering the same question every so often, but little did we know, it created a huge impact on how we would later have toiled and developed relationships with one another and with people around us.

Expressions of love and affection were also very present in our family, and words like "I love you" were exchanged every day. Because both of my parents came from dysfunctional families, they saw to it that they broke the patterns of the past and did things differently for their own children.

As I grew older, I began to better understand many of the valuable life lessons my dad made an effort to teach me. One of the significant lessons that he made me understand, and that I will forever be grateful for, is valuing what it means to have a life partner. He would often remind me, "Vanessa, if there is one decision in life you must never make the mistake of doing, it is in choosing the wrong man you will marry. You can be exact opposites, but your values and principles must be the same. If you do not choose well and you become unhappy in your marriage, it will affect every aspect of your life."

I listened and remembered those words. And so, when I met a man with whom I began to truly fall in love and felt would make a good candidate for a husband, I made him read this book, "Love and Courtship." After that, I realized we did share the same values and wanted the same things in life. That was almost 12 years ago and I am truly blessed to have found my soulmate.

This is why I decided to reprint this book.

Many people nowadays take the word "love" so lightly. It is as if it could be tossed around and thrown out so quickly. But, if two people work at it, take the time and effort to work out their relationship, and allow a true courtship to blossom, these actions will strengthen and build the foundation for lasting love.

Isn't that what we all want? To love and be truly loved!?

Vanessa Garon Vandevoort
July, 2021

Author's Note

I have been counseling people for more than 50 years. During that time, most of the problems I was presented with were about love. Teens in love, couples thinking of marriage, broken relationships, separated couples looking to reconcile, pregnant singles, and people in relationships that they desired to walk away from, but did not know how. The vast majority of people seeking advice from me had then, and still have now, problems with love gone wrong.

What is amazing is that almost all the love problems of the past are the same as those of today. Love is most sought after now as it was in the past. Ironically, love is not more successful today than it was years ago. For countless couples, love isn't what they thought it would be. Many initially believed that their relationships were more than expected, but later had to accept that so much is missing in their love.

In this book, you will find thoughts about courtship and married love. When there is dating and courtship, there is always the chance that more serious outcomes like marriage, courtship, or breakups could happen.

This series of short articles was written as far back as 30 years ago. Much of the advice I would give today is what I would have told my clients over the years.

Bob Garon, July 2021

AN AMAZING LOVE!

IT IS AMAZING HOW CLOSE two people in love can get to each other. Strangers in the beginning, then there comes a total transformation as they merge as one over a period of time. Their love grows to a point where the other is the main concern and the most prized possession in life.

How this change comes about is in many ways a mystery. No one has yet been able to describe the whole process of falling in love in detail. Instead, authors have touched on one or another aspect of this phenomenon of falling in love and what causes that love to grow into something intense.

What strikes me is just one of the many aspects of deep love. DEPENDENCE. There is no question about it. Two people who are deeply in love are very dependent on one another, at least psychologically and emotionally. Webster defines dependence as "the quality or state of being influenced by or subject to another." The word "dependent" is even more specific. Webster defines the adjective as "a) determined or conditioned by another, b) relying on another for support."

When there is dependence, there is an intense degree of conditioning going on. As a lover gets used to his beloved, he becomes conditioned by her, her ways of doing things and how she loves him. Her influence over him grows stronger every day in many ways.

And the reverse is true. She too finds herself being drawn progressively closer and more and more intensely relying on him for emotional support.

As love grows stronger, the ties that mutual dependency create become more binding to the point where it becomes extremely difficult to sever the relationship. And any attempts to do so may cause tremendous pain and discomfort.

There is a kind of security in this dependence. The lover is not alone and that feeling of oneness is impossible to describe. Neither can one who has not experienced deep loving ever appreciate the tremendous feelings of well-being that oneness brings. In everything the lover does, he senses a strong support from his beloved, and there is a great willingness on his part to lend his support for whatever she desires.

The feeling of being loved and appreciated; of being number one in the life of another human being; of having total support from the beloved; all these, creates an unbelievable feeling of comfort and well-being impossible to adequately describe.

The difficulty lies in the pain that strikes at the heart of the lovers when that dependence is broken. In the case of my grandparents, it literally killed. After 64 years of marriage, Grandma passed away. Four months later, Grandpa died of a broken heart and loneliness. He suddenly felt alone. Although surrounded by his children, their love was not comparable to the bond he and Grandma had built over those long years.

And when there is betrayal after having experienced deep love, the pain is that much greater and that much more difficult to bear. Like many things in life, love is a two-edged sword. Its benefits and beauty can become painful memories when they are no longer there

A BALANCED VIEW OF LOVE

A LOVE RELATIONSHIP IS a complicated thing. Like a vast house, it has many rooms and countless little corners. When a relationship is functioning smoothly, the house is in order. When it isn't, there is trouble somewhere. The problems may not extend to every room, and the whole place may not be about to collapse, however, there can be no denying that there are trouble spots.

I say this because we do not usually dissect a relationship. We see it either as doing well or sliding. The reasons for the health or the sickness of a relationship are not very clear to people. The point I want to make here is that, except in a disastrous relationship, there is usually a mixed bag of positives and negatives.

For example, in a certain marriage, the relationship is doing fine in every way, except one. The man is a good provider. He is generally affectionate and loving to his wife and children. He and his spouse are compatible and get along well. Their roles in the home are well defined and adhered to.

HOWEVER, the man had an affair with a woman he does not really love and got caught. Now, the whole question of trust and loyalty is the issue. And the relationship is shaking like crazy because of this one happening. The man still has all the other positives going for him, but the focus is now on his infidelity. In other words, most of the rooms in the house are in order, but fire has broken out in one of them. And this threatens to engulf the whole relationship if it isn't dealt with properly.

In another case, a man may be faithful, a good provider, however, lacking in some other respect. Then, there is the tendency to focus on that weak point and forget much of what is positive in the relationship.

Meanwhile, the whole love or friendship is in trouble because of the inability or the unwillingness of one or both persons to focus on the over-all picture.

This is when the old cliché, "perfection is not of this world" applies. Remember your tendency to idealize relationships and expect perfection or near-perfection from them. This cannot and will not happen.

Instead, realize that there are flaws in every relationship. There are weaknesses that are minuses and there are strengths that are pluses. If the pluses outweigh the minuses, then the overall picture is favorable and you can be grateful for the advantages you enjoy. It is when the reverse is true that trouble arises. When the books of a relationship are running deficits, then, the lovers begin to wonder if it is all worthwhile.

It is most important, especially during a crisis, to focus on the broader view. Keep in mind that there are countless dimensions to a relationship and ALL of them need to be considered. If you can keep a balanced view of your love, chances are you will derive more satisfaction from it than you would otherwise. Also, your decisions about your relationship will be wise

SHOWING CONCERN FOR OTHERS

I OFTEN BUMP INTO PEOPLE who complain that nobody loves them. It is quite clear that such talk is generally untrue and only a ploy to get attention. Self-pity has a way of blinding an individual to some of the most striking realities that surround him.

The truth is that there are many people who do love us very deeply. But, when we get hurt, we forget our friends and the huge emotional investment that they have made. Instead, we mope over our hurt. It's a little like the man with a very healthy body who draws attention to the small cut on his leg. He forgets that he is in splendid physical condition, and begins to worry about his well-being because of the slight wound.

Most people get over these feelings. All that is needed is time for the hurt to subside and new realizations to set in.

There are some people, however, who really believe that nobody loves them, that nobody cares, that the world is a cold place to live in, and that they can never feel responsible concern from anybody. They spend their days sulking in a corner and weeping all over themselves and wishing they had never been born.

Have you ever noticed that kind of people? Remember who they are? Aren't they among those who don't really care about others and who don't really love? And, aren't they mostly found among those who lack warmth and affection and who themselves make our world cold and dreary? Aren't they the ones who often refuse to smile no matter how hard people try to make them do so?

Let's remember that you have to be lovable in order to be loved. If you're a wet blanket and are forever "turning people off," then don't expect to be loved. If you never show interest and concern for others, don't expect them to care for you either. If you're the cold, hard type of person, don't look forward to having all kinds of warm people around you trying to cheer you up and make you smile. You will be sorely disappointed if you do.

Parents, priests, and other brave souls may spend more than their just share of time and emotional effort to turn you the other way. That's their job and their inclination. But, most people will simply walk off and leave you to yourself. They are not out to change the world, but to get what they can from it.

If people don't like you, or are cold to you and if they don't seem to care about you one way or the other, don't look at them, look at yourself. The reason usually lies in the mind and heart of the person who believes the whole world has wronged him.

Do you want people to care for you? Then, show care for them. Do you want them to show you affection?

First show it to them. Do you want to feel people's kindness? Show first your kindness. And would you want to be loved? Then, give love

LOVE THRIVES IN EFFECTIVE COMMUNICATION

PERHAPS THE BEST WAY to poison (and ultimately kill) a fine love relationship or a deep friendship is to cut the lines of communication. Whenever a married couple in trouble comes to me for counseling because their marriage is breaking up on the rocks, I inevitably find that effective communication has, for all practical purposes, ceased.

What goes first is communication. Love is next. It's not the other way around. Love becomes a reality because the channels of communication were opened wide enough to allow true love to take root and grow.

The best way to choke off love is to cut its supply of "oxygen." And what makes love thrive is the transmission of feelings, thoughts, and one's inner self through effective communication.

I can never love you if I cannot communicate myself to you. The old people understand this. They send a girl away in order to separate her from her boyfriend. They know that if the youngsters do not see each other and do not communicate through letters, the days of their love relationship are numbered. And they are right.

Love is like a plant. It needs nourishment and has to be well tended to be productive. Love is also like the stock market. Day by day, it either rises or falls in intensity.

"Falling in love" is only step one. That's easy. You don't even have to try. It just happens. That's why we say people "fall" in love. However, making love grow day by day is really the most difficult job in every love relationship. And good communication is the one factor without which all efforts are doomed to failure.

This is why it is so important that two people who value their love refrain from using such tactics as the famous "silent treatment." Refusing to talk is asking for even greater trouble.

When a problem arises, refusing to communicate only aggravates the situation. When cultivating a love relationship, we spend lots of time just explaining our words and actions so as to avoid useless and unnecessary misunderstandings. The "silent treatment" only serves to increase suspicions of insincerity and ill will.

It is also, I think, a sign of contempt. One day I faced an angry young man in a rehabilitation center and said to him: "Come on, if you're angry with me, say so. Go ahead and curse me if you like."

He looked at me contemptuously and replied softly: "You're not worth it."

It was only when this youngster was able to open up and communicate his thoughts and feelings that he was liberated from the bitterness that was eating him up inside.

It is perhaps significant that some of the most serious mentally disturbed people are characterized by an inability to reach out to others and communicate effectively. I believe that a consistent unwillingness to communicate is the beginning of madness.

WHEN LOVE IS STIFLING

HE WAS A GOOD MAN and a loving father. He valued family life and togetherness. He had cared for his children from the day they were born. And now, as they were entering into adulthood, his caring seemed to increase, especially for his two daughters.

He was protective of them. Some people saw it as more than that. They felt that he was downright possessive. They saw him "running" the lives of his daughters. He kept a tight leash on them. They were closely monitored by him. Their friends were carefully screened. They oftentimes were not granted some of the simplest permissions to do the things that most young ladies take for granted.

The girls themselves were confused. They knew that their father loved them. However, they had difficulty understanding his kind of love. They also could not accept the way he dictated the way they should live their lives. They resented his screening of their friends, not because they had trouble seeing the wisdom of having the right friends, it was more the way he did his screening. He was rude. More than that, he was too much.

The girls felt stifled. They had difficulty living their own lives. They sensed that their father would never let them go. Every time a man approached one of them, Dad would quickly come on the scene and do all in his power to discourage the relationship. They recognized his "love" as being a noose tied around their necks, slowly wringing the life out of them.

Their reactions to the situation were predictable. One day, there was big trouble. One of the girls ran away from home. The father flew into a rage and ordered her back. She refused. Instead, she ran off with a young man who had been secretly courting her. They married and immediately tried to distance themselves from the family.

This happening only served to intensify the father's pressure on his remaining daughter. She soon found herself "guarded" even more securely, and her unhappiness increased with the passing of each day. Until she too, was looking for a way out of her prison. She found it when a man walked into her life. Like her sister, she ran, too.

When a man squeezes too hard, he is likely to destroy the object of his admiration. When he does not allow his beloved to exercise her freedom, he creates a situation that usually ends up in rebellion. Drive a person into a corner and he will push past you and run off. Like the man who admires the beautiful flower. He plucks it and in a few hours it wilts and dies an unsightly death. In loving, we need to allow enough leeway so as not to "kill" the beloved.

Goethe illustrated the point well in his poem "Found."

I walked in the woods
All by myself,
To seek nothing,
That was on my mind.

I saw in the shade
A little flower stand,
Bright like the stars
Like beautiful eyes.

I wanted to pluck it,
But it said sweetly:
Is it to wilt,
That I must be broken?

I pulled it out
With all its roots,
Carried it to the garden
At the pretty house.

And planted it again
In a quiet place,
Now it spreads,
And blossoms forth.

WHAT LOVE CAN DO

A LOT OF THINGS happen when you fall in love. You look and act differently. Instinctively, we know when a couple is in love. There is something about the way they move and look at one another that tells us they are in love. Dr. Bay Birdwhistell, the pioneer in body-language, has discovered that love makes a woman more beautiful.

We meet friends who have known my wife Emmy for many years but have not seen her since we were married. They tell me that she has become more beautiful. There is something about loving that marks a woman's exterior.

Conversely, the unhappy housewife cannot hide her pain and disappointment behind a mask of make-up and a superficial smile. Even the person who is not very observant has a pretty good idea about what she is feeling inside.

The man who is in love feels more alive. He becomes more aware of his appearance. He walks faster and his movements are quicker. There is something about his bearing that telegraphs his feelings of love to the whole world.

Studies have proven that men who are in love tend to be healthier. Those who have unhappy marriages tend to have a higher incidence of heart attacks than the husbands who love their wives and in turn feel the loving concern of their spouses.

Psychologists have discovered that your memory improves when you are in love. The woman in love has an extra-ordinary memory for everything about the man of her dreams. Dr. Malcolm Brenner states that "there's a very close relationship between memory and caring." Our minds, he continues, "are quite selective in what they pay attention to. There's so much going on all around us that we can't comprehend everything at once. We remember the people and things we love."

Another psychologist says that love makes people move physically closer to each other. He concludes that the better a woman likes a man, the closer she gets and vice versa. We all accept that because we can see for ourselves how men and women in love are always touching.

It is also true to say that people in love change. Because I love Emmy, and don't want to hurt her, I have to put a tight rein on my quick temper. I realize that it is only my love for her that oftentimes keeps me from exploding. On the other hand, I can clearly see how Emmy has done a lot of changing herself in order to adapt to some of my ways. Neither one of us would have done so if we didn't love each other.

Bob Garon

Although love does effect a change in people, it can never radically alter their personalities. Many lovers make the fatal mistake of thinking otherwise. The woman who marries an alcoholic, thinking he will be cured by her love, is in for a rude awakening. The young man who believes that his flighty girlfriend will suddenly mature and settle down after their wedding is also setting himself up for a terrible disappointment.

Yes, love does cause changes, but there are some changes that even love cannot bring about. I guess what is important is to know what love can and cannot do. But, that is not easy. If it were so simple, there would be a lot less broken marriages.

LOVE'S CORNERSTONE

ONE OF THE GREAT cornerstones of love is RESPECT. There is nothing more positive, more "love-building" than respect. With it, a relationship grows in depth and strength; without it, there can be only stormy waters ahead.

Perhaps the most vital aspect of respect is the ability to perceive the respected person's needs as being as important as one's own. If I truly respect you, I recognize your needs and, without pressure from you, I will hasten to do whatever I can to see to it that you get satisfaction.

If a wife enjoys working, her man will not force her to remain cooped up in the house because he thinks that a "woman's place is in the home." If he respects her, he will discuss the situation with her and do his best to meet her needs to pursue her career.

Some husbands ride roughshod over the feelings and needs of their wives and, in the process lose the respect of their spouses. The man who dictates who his wife's friends should and should not be, is a tyrant in the home. I have met women who are deeply hurt because of the insensitiveness of their husbands to their needs to have friends.

Bob Garon

The man who dictates to his wife the kind of friends she should have, either does not trust her judgment or is trying to bend her tastes to fit his. In either case, real respect is absent.

The reverse is also true. The wife who constantly nags her man about the kind of people he goes with, does not respect him. Of course, if the husband is hanging around with a group of drunkards and loose living men, I believe she should discuss it thoroughly with him, and more than once if needed.

I don't mean to refer to these obvious situations. There are some much more difficult circumstances which are not so easily resolved. Like the man whose love is flying. His wife may be scared to death every time he happily takes off into the wide blue yonder, but if she understands just how important airplanes are to him, and if she truly respects him, she will support his flying.

I have a couple of friends who have this deep respect for each other and show it through their behavior. After having lived with her husband for many years, the wife knows all his needs and answers to them. He is a tennis buff and since she realizes just how important this is to him, she does all in her power to make sure that his game is as pleasant as possible. She senses what his needs are in other areas as well (career, friends, cultural activities, etc.) and goes out of her way to help him fulfill them.

He, in return, does the same for her. The result is two people trying hard to answer to each other's needs and doing very well at it too. Needless to say that they are madly in love with each other. Undoubtedly, they both feel this way because they are so fulfilled. That's respect

LOVE IS RELATIVE

I WAS ASKED IF I thought he loved her. "I guess it depends on what you mean by love. Love is a relative term. It means different things to different people. I suppose, love is RELATIVE in many ways."

We all have our own points of view. We have formed these opinions and convictions because of many factors: upbringing, education, experience and a lot of our own thinking. We have come to certain conclusions because of our own thought processes, and these thought patterns are different in different people. That is why two people can be talking about love and mean very different things.

When we speak of cooperation, we may not all be talking of the same thing. When asked if we are satisfied with our jobs, we may both answer yes, and yet the meaning of my yes may vary widely from the meaning of your yes.

I think it is important to bear in mind that when we use the same words, we do not always mean the same things. My concept of honesty might not at all be yours. And yet, we both speak of honesty.

This awareness is important for every facet of our lives. However, it is of vital importance when it concerns our relationships, whether in friendship or in marriage.

The concept of loyalty is relative and is given many interpretations. For one, it means no fooling around at all, not at all! For another, it means making sure he comes home AFTER fooling around and under no circumstances leaving one's family.

As long as everybody understands each other, there will be no trouble. However, as soon as the same words begin to mean different things to different people, then you can bet that trouble is just around the corner.

I remember a woman telling me that she was leaving her husband who was a drunkard, a gambler and simply irresponsible. Hardly two years into their marriage, I asked her why she was giving up so soon. Besides, did she know what he was like before marriage? Yes, she knew, but he had promised to change. And, according to her, he had not changed. He maintained that he had changed a lot. He had cut down on his drinking although he still got drunk regularly. He still gambled, but a lot less. The catch was that when she heard him talk about change, she expected real, dramatic changes. He meant minor changes. And since no distinction was made, both went off expecting changes to take place within each context. And when expectations were not met, there were lots of big let-downs and then conflict.

What is important is to make certain you understand what the other is saying and be sure you make yourself understood clearly. Now, this is a whole lot more difficult than meets the eye. Because of our very varied points of view and values; because of our tendency NOT to check out what the other means when he says something; because we assume and presume too much; because of all these, communicating effectively is difficult.

The next time somebody uses a word that is important to you, check it out. Be sure you and him are of one mind as to its meaning. If you can do this, you will avoid a whole lot of unnecessary conflict.

SHOWING ONE'S LOVE

I REMEMBER YEARS AGO preaching at a retreat for young people. During my talk, I was called out of the room. A couple told me that the father of one of the youngsters had just been killed. They asked me to be the one to tell him.

Once inside the small room adjoining the session hall, I did my best to break the news to him as gently as possible. But how gentle can you be in telling a son that his father has just died? Before I had even finished my sentence, the teenager threw up his arms and screamed. Then, as big tears fell from his eyes, he hit the wooden wall with his fist. It was only later that I learned that before he left the house that morning, he had had an encounter with his father. They had parted with harsh words. He did not hate his dad. On the contrary, he loved him deeply. That is what upset him so much. He had died and the son had not yet been able to say "I'm sorry, Dad." Nor was the boy able to hear forgiving words from his father.

I remember a young woman telling me that her Mom was dying of terminal cancer. She wept and said that for a long time she had not told her mother that she loved her. I said, "For your own and your mother's sake, tell her now, before she dies."

Let's face it. Most of our arguments are not that serious when you really get down to it. They are in fact quite petty and not really worth the negative energy we put into them. And when an enemy or somebody with whom we have had a difference is about to die, we want to forgive and receive forgiveness. Perhaps, it is because a dying person is no longer a threat to us. Besides, the thought of carrying the guilt of some unfairness which we showed towards our adversary long after he is dead is worrisome. We really want our conflict to be settled before he dies.

When I leave the house or the office, I always kiss Emmy and tell her I love her. I have done this since the first day of our marriage because I want her to know that should anything happen to me, any conflict we might have had has been forgiven.

Once, I kissed Emmy as I was leaving the office to visit a client. Fifteen minutes later I had a terrible accident which almost killed me. As I lay in the emergency room waiting for Emmy to come to my side, I thought that should I die before she reached me, she would remember that kiss as the last thing that happened in our relationship. That kiss would serve as a healing balm for any conflict that might have remained unresolved.

If you are at a war with a loved one, make your peace **NOW before it is too late!!!**

STEADFAST LOVE

I REMEMBER HER WELL. She was an angry and bitter woman who had once upon a time, loved and been jilted. The man of her dreams had walked away and married another. Her deep involvement with him and the pain of the subsequent breakup and alienation had made her a cold person, unwilling to love again. And, that is exactly what happened. She lived out the rest of her life alone and angry.

There are those who get burned once in love and vow never to love again. And they don't. Others get hurt in love and somehow go on to love again in spite of former disappointments and setbacks. The difference in outlook on similar happenings is dependent on attitudes. Attitudes that were instilled in us over the years. Attitudes that we cultivated and nourished throughout our lives.

There are those whose dreams were shattered and who gave up dreaming altogether. Their broken dreams caused so much personal hurt that they became fearful of dreaming again lest they suffer once again. On the other hand, there are those who, in spite of repeated setbacks, continued to dream and dream until, through hard work, their dreams began to come true. The former became beaten dreamers, the latter emerged victorious.

I remember a woman who gave up on God because she said her prayers were not answered. God had not given her what she wanted, and she turned against Him because He was not a yes-man.

Then, there are those who go on praying no matter what the outcome. Their faith is such, that regardless of what finally happens, they believe that God is their guide; that He watches over them; and that their destinies are in His hands.

Again, the difference in outlook is the product of an attitude of prayer. Attitudes are so important in our lives because they pretty much determine our behavior patterns. Know a man's attitudes and you can very well predict his actions.

I came across this piece recently that very well illustrates some strong and positive values.

STEADFAST HEART

I've dreamed many dreams that never came true.
I've seen them vanish at dawn,
But I've realized enough of my dreams, Thank God,
To make me want to dream on.

I've prayed many prayers when no answer came,
Though I waited patient and long,
But answers have come to enough of my prayers
To make me keep praying on.

I've trusted many a friend that failed,
And left me to weep alone,
But I've found enough of my friends, true blue
To make me keep trusting on.

I've sown many seeds that fall by the way
For the birds to feed upon,
But I've held enough golden sheaves in my hands
To make me keep sowing on.

I've drained the cup of disappointment and pain
And gone many ways without song,
But I've sipped enough nectar from the roses of life
To make me want to live on.

GROWTH PATTERNS IN LOVE

THERE ARE MANY CAUSES for men and women calling it quits after a long and seemingly solid relationship. However, there is one reason for breaking up that is more common than anyone suspects. I refer to the intellectual gap that exists between a man and a woman.

We are all hopefully in the process of growing: emotionally, spiritually, psychologically and intellectually. However, people do not grow uniformly. Some grow so swiftly that it's scary. Scary because they are changing so rapidly that you cannot really understand what is going on inside them. And unless you are growing equally fast, you will get left behind. Others grow very slowly, almost at a snail's pace. They are pretty much the same today as they were years ago. Not very much has happened to change them. Keeping up with them is a simple matter.

There are of course countless factors that determine one's growth pattern. But, there is one which I would like to focus on here: EXPOSURE. The executive who spends his day in intellectually stimulating and challenging conversations with bright men and women is growing a whole lot more than his wife who stays at home and takes care of the home and the children. Hers is a small world of child's talk, report cards, grocery talk and cooking. While she is devoting herself to the home and her growing brood, she oftentimes ends up falling far behind her husband intellectually.

As time passes, the intellectual distance between them becomes a problem. It is not something that happens quickly. On the contrary, the situation slowly evolves (most often after a number of years) until it creeps up on a couple almost imperceptibly. Then, one day, he wakes up and comes to the conclusion that he no longer finds his wife intellectually stimulating. And for many genuinely successful men, intellectual stimulation is a very real need. They feel bored when having to do without it regularly.

If a man has risen quickly in his career, there is a possibility that his swift movement up has broadened his horizons considerably. And thus, there is the danger of a growing gap between him and the woman he has been keeping at home all those years.

Some women sense what is happening and attempt to break out. They want to keep up. They feel that they are not growing and are being left behind. If the husband insists on the status quo, there is trouble. The woman may insist on pursuing a career, or even going back to school. If the husband will not allow it and she eventually gives in, she most likely will go on resenting him for "keeping me down."

Some of these women also sense that there is a widening gap developing between them and their husbands. It is only a feeling, but it is a feeling that tells them that they are losing ground.

Many married executives fall in love with women whom they find intellectually as well as sexually stimulating. Oftentimes, the first is more significant than the second. After all, sexual gratification is easy enough to find, especially when one has the money.

It is sad how sometimes a wife's devotion to her home, her children and her husband is not enough; how goodwill and noble intentions fall short of what is needed to keep their love vibrant and meaningful; how all she has been doing over the years turns out to be "not enough."

By the way, the same can be said of successful career women whose husbands have also failed to keep up to them. Many of them oftentimes experience the same needs and find that they have so thoroughly outgrown their husbands that they see their once exciting relationship becoming dull.

THE HEART HAS REASONS

SHE HAD JUST BROKEN UP with the man she loved. Her head told her that the relationship was such that it could not work out. She had gone through a lot of inner processing. Finally, after much talking, much thinking and much apprehension on the part of both, they decided to call it quits.

It was a friendly separation. No harsh words. No anger. No shouting. No arguments. Just a mutual agreement to give each other the freedom to pursue other options. Maybe the reason why parting was so hurting was that it was done so gently. They were still friends. It was like having him just a little bit. Somehow, deep in her heart, she wanted more of him.

Yet, logic had prevailed. There were simply too many solid reasons which lined up against continuing the relationship. Yet, the pain was still there. The French, I think, have an expression that goes something like this: "The heart has reasons that the head can never understand." Although her decision made a lot of sense, still the hurt was there.

She had given so much to the relationship and now it seemed to amount to nothing except a lot of memories.

She had nurtured high expectations and now she was left with a bagful of unfulfilled expectations. The disappointments were great.

Now that the decision to part had been made, she was paying the price. And the tag was high. Perhaps, what was most difficult was forgetting. Putting it all behind was easier said than done.

The split had created a vacuum in her life. There was a kind of emptiness that longed to be filled. She was alone now, and she sorely missed the companionship of her boyfriend. Even if her love had been stormy, at least, there was someone. There were nights when she cried herself to sleep.

With the passing of time, the wounds in her heart slowly began to heal. It was a painful process, but one which she felt would somehow bring her relief. It did. After a bucket of tears and many months of adjusting, she finally was back to "normal."

Breakups are always difficult whether one is the initiator or not. There is that sense of loss which is present to a greater or lesser degree. And even if one has fallen out of love and is saying goodbye, even then, there is a kind of feeling of betrayal that prevails.

Time, more than anything else, is the great healer. One can reason, share with friends, pray to God. All this is good, but still, time is what is needed.

Time and the desire to put the past behind and start anew. Time and the faith in oneself that another day will bring another love. Time and the belief that tomorrow will bring an even more exciting relationship.

THE DIMENSION OF LOVE

VALENTINE'S DAY! It is the day that commemorates the martyrdom of the Christian soldier St. Valentine. It is also the day which focuses on love. Lovers and friends are sending little cards with big red hearts. Countless messages of love are being distributed everywhere.

Valentine's Day is also an especially sad day for those whose love relationships are in trouble or have failed completely. The festivities and the red hearts seen everywhere are painful reminders of what could have been but isn't. The memories of love that did not work out are extremely difficult to erase. Valentine's Day only seems to serve to resurrect them.

When we experience love, it is something we are not about to forget quickly or easily. Love makes its mark upon the heart. When it is true, it is overwhelming. It is capable of turning a person's life around with the snap of a finger. It has caused lovers to endure the most difficult situations in its name.

If a man or woman is without love, there is a vacuum, an emptiness which dominates. Life takes on less meaning. Love is what allows us to grow in many dimensions, all at the same time. It allows us to perfect the art of giving. It teaches us how to receive the goodness and kindness of others. It causes the nobility within us to surface. Love moves us to forget ourselves so that others may benefit. It makes sacrifice appealing and worthwhile.

I remember a young man who was deeply in love with a beautiful woman. Since he was among the poorest of the poor, he could not even afford transportation expenses to visit her. So, early Sunday morning, he would begin walking to her house. At about noon, he would arrive. After two or three hours with her, he had to leave her for the long walk home. When I remarked how hard his walking must be, he answered simply:

"On my way to see her, I keep thinking about what I want to tell her, for I know our time together will be short. On my way back, I keep thinking about what we talked about. This way, I really hardly notice the distance I have to walk."

It is amazing what a person will do for love!

St. Valentine was asked to give up his faith or die. He preferred to face death rather than deny his God. Consequently, he was executed. The love he showed for the Almighty is classic. It is the ultimate expression of love.

We may never be called upon to give up our lives in such a dramatic fashion. However, there is no question in my mind that two people loving deeply ARE giving their lives to each other. Their loyalty and concern spell out a dedication that knows no bounds of giving. Instead of finding death, they discover new life in their giving. They find fulfillment and meaning in the very act of giving.

DIFFERENT CONCEPTS OF LOVING

A PSYCHOLOGIST ONCE COMPARED married life to the stage: "Love, for the woman, is itself the drama; for the man, it is the intermission."

For the man, love is a very powerful impulse, very sexual in nature. It forms only part of his sphere of interests. In other words, a man feels that there is more to life than loving. There is his job, sports, politics and the creative arts. There also is the challenge and the adventure of competition.

On the other hand, love, for a woman, constitutes a whole way of life. It is not a part-time activity for her. Everything she does, she does out of love. Otherwise, her life becomes stained with bitterness. A woman looks at life as something that is all-encompassing and all-embracing.

For her, love means a permanent level of affection. Loving becomes almost an obsession. To her there is no "time out" from love. In fact, she stands in mortal fear of ever having to experience a decline in the affection she receives from the loved one.

This is why a wife always longs to be with her husband and wants to know all about his work, even though she understands little or nothing about it. And when her husband does not want to talk about it because he is aware that it is beyond her, and not necessarily because he no longer loves her, she gets hurt and begins to suspect something is radically wrong with their marriage. She cannot understand that her husband does not care to talk just for the sake of talking. He cannot comprehend the fact that it is not understanding his work that is so important to his wife. It is rather his time and the attention he gives that is vital to her.

A woman counts the hours the man gives her. The man gives more importance to what is put in the hours. A woman needs to hear tender words from the man she loves. She has to feel, and constantly needs to remain secure. Although a man needs to feel his woman's love too, he is more readily satisfied with knowing that his wife/sweetheart loves him. He needs to feel, and to be continuously reassured, is not as deep as that of his female counterpart.

If her husband goes off to watch a basketball game without her, she may feel he doesn't love her any longer. If he shows interest in other things, she thinks he is no longer interested in her. In fact, the man loves her deeply, but doing everything together does not come into his concept of love. He believes he can love his wife and still care very much for other matters. In short, his wife is not everything to him.

These different concepts of loving create confusion and sometimes wreak havoc on marriages and courtships.

We often witness the tragic spectacle of two people madly in love but wildly battling each other for lack of understanding of the basic differences in the male and female concepts of loving.

Not that the woman's way of loving is better. Nor is it a question of who's right and who's wrong. The truth lies in the fact that both concepts are simply different. Once a couple understands this and accepts it, you can be sure that they will avoid many traps and pitfalls that less mature couples inevitably fall into.

GROWING LOVE

THE OTHER DAY, I was telling Emmy that my love for her had grown more intense over the past five years. As I said that, I stopped and wondered, what exactly did I mean by that? We always talk about our love growing, and yet, what does a growing love mean? Does it mean a magnification of that feeling we first felt when we initially fell in love? Is it that same love feeling multiplied a number of times? Or does growing love mean new and added dimensions to an already existing love base?

I tend to think that it is the last. When I look at HOW my love for Emmy has grown, I find that I have discovered new dimensions to her that cause me to constantly re-evaluate her and appreciate her more and more.

For example, I suspected that she was a strong woman when I married her. In fact, this was an asset that particularly attracted me to her. However, as I watch her handle problems and difficulties, there is an ever-increasing awareness that I had underestimated her strength. Many new dimensions of her capacity to deal with hardship and disappointment have surfaced. This awareness has made me realize that I have a more powerful woman than I had originally suspected. Thus, she becomes even more precious to me. Consequently, my love for this aspect of her has grown.

The same is true of the WAY she loves me. I have never doubted her love for me; however, she has found so many ways to express this love that I have discovered new dimensions in her again. Thus, my love for her has grown as I perceive her to be even more valuable to me than I ever before thought.

As a person understands that the woman he loved this much is really worth so much more, his love increases proportionately. There is a rising appreciation for the beloved. And as the lover discovers more and more positive dimensions in the beloved, the appreciation level rises and so does the level of love.

The reverse is also true. The more negative the dimensions one discovers in the beloved, the more the appreciation level falls. And subsequently, the intensity of love cools. Because the lover's eyes are open to the negatives which seem to outweigh the positives, he begins to feel cheated. He slowly becomes convinced that he made the wrong decision in committing himself in the first place. This realization causes him to start backing away from his original commitment. It is the beginning of dying love.

If you want to measure your love, try quantifying your appreciation for your beloved. If you want to know if your love is growing or dying, establish whether or not your new awareness of each other are more positive than negative. If so, chances are your love is on the upswing. If, on the other hand, you see more negatives than positives, your love is probably in a dive.

44

SECURITY IN MATURED LOVE

I REMEMBER WITH FONDNESS, and a sense of awe, the marriage of my grandparents. They were very young when they walked down the aisle. He 17 and she 16. They had 16 children. Life was very hard. They were poor most of the time. Only in the sunset years of their lives did they enjoy a degree of material ease and comfort. One day, they celebrated their 64th wedding anniversary.

They were a happy couple because their love was of the deeply matured kind. There was something about their relationship that gave me the feeling that it was as solid as a block of marble. They were unbelievably comfortable with each other. It was as if neither one could surprise the other; so well did they know each other.

I remember asking Grandma if she ever got bored with Grandpa. She said she didn't. Their love was such that when she died, Grandpa followed her four months later. They were very loyal to each other. Never did I ever hear even a faint whisper of doubt about Grandpa's fidelity. He was a "one-woman man."

In new love, there are always high hopes and great expectations. Some of these hopes are unreasonably high and some of the expectations unrealistic. This is why new love is so often such a big disappointment. There is excitement not only about what is, but about the joy that is to come. And when the expectations remain unfulfilled and the hopes are dashed to the ground, of course there is unhappiness.

In matured love like that of my grandparents, there is security. Security in knowing and in having experienced the realization of some of these hopes. Security in understanding that even if other hopes and expectations never materialized, their love nevertheless grew in depth and meaning. Security in having lived together through all kinds of crises, and in knowing that these problems only served to further cement their relationship. Security in the confidence felt because of their ability to overcome and grow stronger despite trials and tribulations.

This kind of security, new love can never have because it has not yet been tested. New-found love experiences fear and doubt. Fear that it might lose what it has. Doubt about its potentials to withstand the inevitable stormy times that are sure to surface somewhere on the horizon.

New lovers sense that their love can lift them to the most distant star or drop them into the deepest depths. This at once excites and terrifies. However, the thrill, the possibility of soaring to great heights, causes them to take the risk.

Matured love is different. It has taken its chances and WON. It is enjoying the fruits of victory. Like victorious, battle-hardened soldiers, mature lovers look forward to the future with confidence because of their track record. They are confident of tomorrow because they were successful yesterday and remain so today.

The excitement of matured love is more of the serene kind. There is a degree of calmness and quiet about it that is absent in new-found love. If new-found love is like hard rock music, matured love is more like classical music. It isn't that one is better than the other. It is just that they are different. Different stages of loving.

And, if new love is to survive, it must evolve into the matured kind. If it fails to do so, it is destined to die.

SLOW- GROWTH LOVE

THERE ARE MANY YOUNG women who, no matter how hard they try, never seem to succeed in love. Perhaps it is because they are in too much of a hurry to fall in love. Perhaps they do not understand that love is like a plant of slow growth that takes a long time to blossom. Perhaps they do not realize that before there is authentic love, there must be deep friendship. And deep friendship doesn't just happen. It must be worked at… and worked at hard.

I remember a meaningful song I enjoy listening to. It speaks of a beautiful friendship between a man and a woman. It tells how they treated one another as brother and sister. It recounts how they did things together and just simply enjoyed each other's company. And it describes how one evening, both of them understood that, "this was the end of a beautiful friendship and the beginning of love."

Some women move very quickly and rather recklessly into a relationship. There is a whirlwind of parties, movies, sweet words, promises and sexual involvement. Everything… except deep friendship.

What these women do not understand is that SERIOUS men look for more in a woman than just fun. What they fail to comprehend is that men, whether they be matured or not, easily get bored with women. Unless there is more to their affair than partying and movie going and just having fun, there can be no lasting relationship of any worth.

Unless these women come to the realization that love is an art that is not easily mastered, they will go on and on looking for easy romance. They will forever be searching for that satisfying love that will always elude them. They will, again and again, think that with each new relationship they have finally come to the end of their quest for true love. And, after repeated failures and disillusionments, they will grow weary and finally succumb to discouragement.

They might even give up their desire for deep and lasting love and settle for what momentary pleasures and superficial relationships might bring. When that day dawns, these restless women begin to walk the long road downhill. And, unless someone reaches out to them in authentic and sincere friendship, they never find their way back.

BETTER TO HAVE LIVED AND LOVED

THEY WERE SUCH A happy couple. After four years of marriage, it was as if the honeymoon was just beginning. The level of caring, of affection remained high. In fact, it was climbing steadily. She considered herself to be the luckiest woman in the world and her joy knew no bounds. Conflicts were few and far between. They were an almost perfect couple, she thought. Their thinking was pointed in the same direction. It was not that they were clones, but they came from similar backgrounds. Their values and interests were pretty much the same. And so, it was easy for their love to take root and grow swiftly.

In the midst of all this happiness, disaster struck. One day, they discovered that he had an incurable cancer. The shock became more intense as reality sank deeply into their hearts and minds. At first, she simply did not want to believe it. She talked to the physician again and again. The same answer always came back. Her husband was given less than a year to live. Only a miracle could save him. Of course miracles were possible, but not likely.

Now, this woman who was the recipient of such bountiful joy fell into deep depression. Sadness enveloped her like a cloud. She would lose the object and the source of her love. She would be left alone to fend for herself. If she had never experienced so much joy, then doing without would be a simple matter. However, after all the high levels of happiness, the prospect of losing it all was extremely hurting.

Next, she became angry at God for allowing this to happen. Angry at the world and society. She was not sure why, but she was angry nevertheless. Her anger grew at first and then subsided. Then, came a feeling of resignation and helplessness. There was nothing she could do about the situation. Although still terribly sad, she decided to make the most of the remaining time.

His feelings were much the same, only more intense and with more dimensions. He was staring death in the face. He was young. In his early thirties. And his life was coming to an inevitable close, just as he was beginning to live. It all seemed so unfair. After experiencing great sadness and a lot of inner turmoil, he too, began to feel resigned to his fate.

More than that, he started to prepare himself for his journey. He had always made time for God and so he felt prepared spiritually. And as he weakened physically, he felt himself growing stronger in his faith. He put his finances and business in order. More than anything else, he wanted more time with her.

Now, every minute was important. Time was at once, his worst enemy and his most valuable possession.

Their love grew rapidly with the passing of each day. They valued their moments together. Life was reduced to the barest essentials for them. In fact, they were amazed at how easy it was to get along without all the concerns they used to have. As the end drew near, their love for each other seemed to expand beyond all bounds. Theirs was a mixture of tremendous joy and deep sadness.

Their love provided the happiness. The reality of impending separation caused the sadness. When the end did come, it was as beautiful as can be under the circumstances. Death had exacted its terrible price. But love had dispensed its unbelievable rewards too.

All in all, it was better to have lived and loved rather than to have merely lived.

EDITING IN LOVE

WHEN A MAN MEETS a stranger, he does a lot of editing. He is careful about what he says and how he says it, lest he offend and cause himself to be rejected. The same is true of lovers during courtship, except that both are editing at a very high intensity level.

What is editing? It is the opposite of spontaneity. It means choosing one's words. It means doing everything possible to carefully express one's thoughts so that one will not be misunderstood. There is always a degree of tension while editing. Should this be said this way or that? Or should it be said at all? If I say this, will be I misunderstood? What if he interprets what I say in a manner that will compromise me?

And so, the editing goes on. Careful with his words, the editor is tense, ever alert, weighing the implications of his words before speaking them. He is not spontaneous because he cannot afford to be.

New-found lovers are editors during the early part of their relationship. They need to be because of the fragile nature of their love. The trust level is low and could easily collapse under the weight of suspicion. The intensity of their loving leaves much to be desired because it is still in its infancy. Consequently, such a love can easily be shattered. The personal involvement of the lovers is not yet very strong thus allowing one to walk away without much ado.

So, it is important to edit not only one's words, but also one's behavior. During courtship, lovers are on their very best behavior. Because they are trying hard to impress each other favorably, they do and say things in order to show themselves worthy of the beloved.

Although this is needed in the beginning, it should occur less and less often in the times that follow. Editing is a protective device. That is good. However, it also causes a person oftentimes to be less than honest in what he says and does. Just as the film editor cuts out those scenes that are not very well done, so too does the lover attempt to gloss over those parts of his life that he thinks will have a negative effect on his beloved. He is trying to win her and anything that does not promote that end, is edited out.

The danger of editing is obvious. Getting to know the editor truly will be that much more difficult since his words and behavior are edited. Hence, the beloved is going to have to read between the lines in order to fully understand him. And, if unsuccessful at deciphering his editing, the beloved may marry the man and know him later on in an "unedited" manner. That could come as a rude awakening.

Unless the level of editing progressively drops and eventually disappears altogether, a couple can never achieve that level of spontaneity that is essential for deep and meaningful love. When one or both spouses suddenly wake up after marriage and feel they have been cheated; when a spouse says that "the woman I courted is not the woman I married"; when there are plenty of surprises after marriage; then, it is because the couple never got past the heavy editing stage.

FALLING IN LOVE IN SLOW MOTION

"One does not fall in or out of love. One grows in love."
—Leo Buscaglia

I REMEMBER A SONG by Nat King Cole in which he sings about a friendship slowly and imperceptibly turning into love. We are quick to talk about "falling in love." Well, if we do fall, it is in slow motion.

There is of course, swift and almost instantaneous attraction. When a man meets a beautiful woman and is immediately drawn to her, even before she says a word, he must be careful not to call this love. Males and females, by nature, get attracted to one another. Beautiful females and handsome males may, at first sight, be more attractive. However, there is a world of difference between attractiveness and love. A person may get hurt badly if he or she is unable to distinguish one from the other.

The woman who believes she has "fallen" in love at first sight is walking a dangerous path. Because she is so sure that she is deeply in love (even if she is not) she is not careful about looking critically into her relationship. She does not question nor does she allow herself to doubt. And, anyone who is thinking of a life-long commitment should certainly question. She should also permit all her doubts to surface so they can be dealt with and erased.

Love is a plant of slow growth. It rarely flares up and takes strong root overnight. It must be nourished and cultivated in fertile soil if it is to blossom. Love is not a miracle plant. It does not grow well anywhere and everywhere. It needs a special kind of environment. It calls for careful nurturing.

People who are quick to "fall in love" usually end up just as quickly falling out of love. Loving is a multi-dimensional experience, one that cannot be had in a day. Any week-old or month-old love is indeed something fragile.

It may be spectacular in its quick initial intensity, but if it is to become lasting it must have a reservoir of slow-burning coals. And this can only happen if it has burned for some time.

What is tricky about loving is that it is such a heavy mixture of so many things. It is influenced by countless factors: one's prevailing mood; all kinds of emotional and psychological needs; even material needs. It is so difficult to measure these factors and weigh their influence on love.

This is why there is so much confusion in love relationships. People feel strong feelings. These feelings evolve. They vary in their levels of intensity. They sometimes disappear altogether only to surface again later on.

Knowing that love (real, deep and authentic love) is more complex than meets the eye helps. It helps because when one understands that his approach reflects his understanding, he does not expect quick answers. On the contrary, he braces himself for a lot of soul-searching. He looks for quality in his relationship. And because he looks hard, he usually finds it.

HOW INTENSE IS YOUR LOVE?

WHEN TWO PEOPLE GET married, they vow to love each other "for better, for worse, for richer, for poorer, in sickness and in health, until death do us part." But this vow does not indicate the intensity of their love. Persons in love rarely try to measure the intensity of their loving. And, since love is so difficult to quantify even under the best of circumstances, when a man and a woman marry all they know is that they "are in love."

Although not often talked about, the intensity of their love is of vital importance. It is what will determine how well their marriage will withstand the trials and pressures that are certain to come along sooner or later.

People whose love is only superficial, and who decide to spend the rest of their lives together are in for a lot of unpleasant surprises. As the crises come bursting into their marriage, the intensity of their love is not enough to handle them and they are overwhelmed.

This is why some marriages are so short-lived. They never really stood much of a chance from the very start. The foundations were built on sand.

The quality of love is what keeps two people together even when the wind blows and the rains threaten to erode all they have built.

The other day, I spoke to a young woman whose marriage lasted exactly three months. She is a nice woman. Kind and patient, she could have made a man a good wife. But the guy she "fell in love with" was the wrong man. It wasn't that he was bad. He also had many sterling qualities. It was just that the two of them were incompatible from the beginning. There were too many areas of conflict. And when these conflicts broke out, they caused far more pressures than their flimsy love could bear.

Inevitably, their love took a heavy battering and began to sour. In the end, there was so much hostility between them that separation was seen as a welcome relief by both of them.

Whenever people tell you that they are in love, believe it. Undoubtedly, they are. However, ask yourself what is the degree of intensity of their love. That, of course, is not easy to determine, yet, it is possible to get an idea of the depth of their love.

If both possess a high degree of maturity, they deserve a lot of points. If their courtship has been serious and of a long enough duration, their chances increase. If they have characters and personalities which balance each other, the odds climb in their favor. If they have much in common, do things together, and believe in pretty much the same values; then, their love is well-founded and should be capable of withstanding a lot of heavy crises. This is the kind of love that lasts over the years through thick and thin.

"PROJECTING" IN LOVE

NOT ALL MEN HAVE what it takes to love deeply. All have the potential, but potential is one thing and the actualization of that potential is something else. What do you look for when trying to determine those people with little ability to love? Having few friends is one indication. Excessive ambition, another.

Whenever you meet someone who seems to constantly echo the complaint: "Nobody loves me; nobody understands me," you can suspect that this individual may not be in a very good position to love.

A man who feels unloved is usually a person who isn't doing much loving himself because he's too busy wallowing in self-pity. The individual who feels that nobody understands him ordinarily has very little understanding of others. Oftentimes, he doesn't even attempt to understand other people because he doesn't care enough to invest the time and effort.

Usually, this person is doing a lot of PROJECTING. Projection is something we all get into once in a while. Some people, however, make it a way of life.

A noted psychologist ably describes projection: "We frequently suspect in ourselves unpleasant characteristics which we hate to face. Unconsciously, we save ourselves this disagreeable experience by seeing these traits in others, of whom we can then comfortably disapprove. We PROJECT the trait." How often, in an argument, does the man who feels rage rising in him shout at his adversary: "What are you getting so angry about?"

When one member of a group is doing all the talking and someone else tries to get a word in, how often have we seen the talker accuse the other of monopolizing the conversation? Or accuse someone else of being dogmatic when he himself has offered more opinions with greater certainty and less documentation than anyone present? These are all familiar instances of projection.

In the same way, somebody who feels nobody loves him is most likely not loving anybody and is simply projecting.

Another sign may come as a surprise to you. It is the ability to say "No." The girl who cannot say "no" may look very loving since she tries to please everybody. The fact of the matter is that she (and others like her) may not love anybody deeply. Because she must please at all costs, she cannot bear the conflict that is always part of the price of a meaningful relationship. Besides, she is too busy buying everyone's affection.

The truth is that people like her feel an acute sense of unworthiness. They cannot really believe they are lovable. Nor do they think themselves capable of great love. Consequently, like a butterfly they flutter from one person to another forever in search of a little bit of sweetness to make their bitter lives bearable.

64

ONENESS OF HEART AND MIND

LOVE IN ITS DEEPEST meaning calls for the oneness of heart and mind. This desire for togetherness grows stronger as love intensifies. And, when love begins to die, the desire to stay close fades. And, when love is dead, there remains only the desire to separate.

I remember my grandparents. They were married 64 years. And when Grandma died, Grandpa became terribly depressed. In less than 90 days, he too was dead. The doctor said he died of a broken heart.

I have just read of a sad but touching incident that happened in America some time ago. It is sad because it ended in deaths. It is touching because of the deep love that inspired the deaths. Let me share it with you.

NORTH FORT MYERS, Fla. (AP) - Julia Saunders, 81, had her hair done. Her husband, Cecil, 85, collected the mail one final time and paused to chat with a neighbor. Inside their mobile home, they carefully laid out a navy blazer and a powder-blue dress.

After lunch, the Saunders drove to a rural corner of Lee County and parked. As cows grazed in the summer heat, the couple talked, then Cecil Saunders shot his wife of 60 years in the heart and turned the gun on himself.

Near the clothes they had chosen to be buried in, the couple had left a note:

"Dear children, this we know will be a terrible shock and embarrassment. But we see it, as one solution to the problem of growing old. We greatly appreciate your willingness to try to take care of us.

After being married for 60 years, it only makes sense for us to leave this world together because we loved each other so much!"

On the floorboard of the car, Cecil and Julia Saunders had placed typewritten funeral instructions, and the telephone numbers of their son and daughter. They draped the Chevrolet's seat with a shower curtain and wool blanket so their blood would leave no permanent stain.

Then they consummated their suicide pact.

Julia's dimming eyesight, heart congestion and a stroke had driven Cecil to place his ailing wife in a nursing home earlier that year. But she became hysterical over what she thought was poor care there, and Cecil brought her home.

"You never saw him without her," said Vera Whittimore, 67. "If there ever was true love, they had it. I think they were just tired of living and couldn't wait for God to take them."

From inside a green washrag, Cecil unwrapped the revolver he had purchased eight days before. In its chamber were six bullets. Both husband and wife plugged their ears with twists of cotton to muffle the sound of shots.

Cecil reached over and held the Smith & Wesson inches from his wife's breast. Julia closed her brown eyes behind metal-rimmed glasses.

Cecil fired twice.

One bullet pierced his wife's heart, and blood poured onto her red-and-white-print dress. Her head fell backward against the car seat, and she died in seconds.

Cecil watched life leave her. Then, as he had promised his wife, he pointed the revolver at his shirt pocket and pulled the trigger one final time.

LOVE'S PRICE TAG

WHENEVER WE RUN INTO a couple that strikes us as having an unusually intimate relationship, we marvel at the beauty of it all. We also think about how lucky the two are to have "found each other."

Finding each other is only part of the story. True, it is a critical part. Every relationship must begin with the right ingredients. Maturity, compatibility and a healthy environment: all this is a must, if a love is to have any kind of chance at success.

It does not at all end here though. Far too many of us believe that love is an automatic sort of device that once activated, produces a steady stream of happiness. Not true. This is a myth and a very dangerous one at that. It perpetuates the thinking that once two persons have fallen in love, they are in love to stay. Nothing could be farther from the truth. And yet, it is amazing how prevalent this thinking is in the minds of people. It is like seeing love as a drug, a pill that, once taken, does its work without any need to further effort.

The truth of the matter is very different. A closer examination of those rare "beautiful relationships" will show that there is nothing automatic about intense loving. If a couple wants to have a dynamic, a vital kind of love, they will have to make up their minds to work hard at it from the very beginning. And then, they must know that their love will need constant and careful nurturing.

We have all seen beautiful properties that have striking gardens. We are amazed at them, but are quick to note how well they are maintained. You cannot have a fine garden unless you put lots of time into it.

If this is so, when it concerns gardens, how much more does a love relationship need time and effort to keep it at its peak? Plants are a whole lot less complex than people. They are more predictable, and much easier to care for.

The problem with most lovers is that this kind of thinking tends to lull them into the sleep of carelessness. They get to thinking that their love is now and forever and nothing can, nor will break it up. In short, they take their relationship for granted. From there, it is only a few short steps to the beginning of trouble.

It was the Lord who warned the master of the house to keep watch over his house lest the thieves break into it in the middle of the night. In the same way, it is essential for lovers to guard their love. They must not take each other for granted. They have to be quick to react to conflict that might creep into their love. They should be aware that there are countless traps and pitfalls that lay in the path of even the most solid love. And, unless they are watching for them, they should understand that the tremendous joy they now experience can become a memory of the past. And memories of this sort are bitter because they are reminders of the beauties of a love that might still be, had it not been lost.

My Dad used to tell me that "anything worthwhile does not come free." He used to get terribly irritated when I spent time looking for an easy way out when there was none. "Bobby" he would say, "you've got to pay the price, so pay it, or forget about it."

The price tag on a beautiful love relationship states it clearly. It reads: "Hard work."

MONITORING THE LEVEL OF LOVE

A WHILE AGO, I WAS watching my wife Emmy water the plants in our backyard. A thought struck me. Whereas outside the wall, everything is beginning to turn a dull brownish color, our garden is a lush green. The reason is obvious: water. That life-giving substance is plentiful and so, our little garden is an oasis.

Then, I thought of marriage and how, in spite of the trials it sometimes generates, it is possible to overcome all as long as there is LOVE. This may sound obvious to you, but it is not as simple as it seems. When something goes wrong in a marriage, many people look everywhere for all kinds of reasons for the breakdown. Oftentimes, nobody wants to believe that the answer to the problem lies in dying love. Perhaps, it is because no one wants to believe that such a thing is actually happening.

When the level of love begins to fall, then you can expect all kinds of problems to arise where there were none before. Like a sickness that debilitates slowly, dying love attacks a relationship in an almost imperceptible manner. At first, it is hardly noticeable. Then, as the conflicts and tensions grow more intense, the suspicion that perhaps love is dying becomes more obvious.

Bob Garon

In my counseling sessions with couples in trouble, one of the first things I try to do is determine the level of love, or, more often than not, if there is any love left at all. If there is little remaining, I know that the chances of reversing a deteriorating situation are slim. If there is lots of love, then the chances of fixing things up are excellent. If, however, love is dead, then, the prognosis is poor. The chances of changing things for the better are almost non-existent. Either the couple goes on suffering and stumbling from one conflict to another, or the partners get down to the business of seriously courting each other all over again. Something has to be done to fan the fires of love once again. Otherwise, the chances of success are nil.

Love is what makes a marriage click. It is what allows individuals to be tolerant of each other. It is what makes it easy to forgive and heal hurt feelings. It is the cement that binds. Take away love and all you have left is a shell of a relationship. Those who believe they can still keep a relationship going without love are sorely mistaken. Perhaps, there will be some kind of peaceful co-existence for a while. However, in the end, it will all come to nothing.

If only couples were more careful in monitoring the level of their love, they would be better suited to foresee the oncoming problems. Instead of going into all kinds of fruitless exercises to determine their problems, they would concentrate on increasing their love for one another. And, as the intensity of their love increases once again, the difficulties they are having will lessen proportionately.

VITAL ASPECT OF LOVE

THERE ARE MANY DIMENSIONS to falling in love. A lot of things happen when one feels himself becoming almost inevitably drawn to another human. Love is so powerful that it moves where it will. It happens to the strongest people, in the most unusual of circumstances, and oftentimes in the most unsuspecting moments. There is a deep mystery about love that is unfathomable. But, it is in this unknown factor that lies its appeal and allure.

Perhaps, the most commonly recognized aspect of love is the strong desire to give to the beloved. This is a universally acknowledged fact. Where love exists, there will be found the instinctive urge to give. More than that, there is a drive to give, a force that wants to know no limits and that must be held within bounds by reason. The great generosity of the man in love is perceived by many to be extreme and even foolish. This is because the old saying, "the heart has reasons that reason cannot understand," is very true.

There is, however, another facet of loving that most lovers do not consciously understand and are less than willing to accept. And that is, the receiving aspect implied in the state of being loved. I said "receiving" and not taking. The word "take" has a certain ring about it that implies violence and has no place in love. If I am truly loved, then, I am on the receiving end of many kinds of benefits. This is a necessary condition for a true love relationship.

Although most people will argue the point with me, I maintain that love can be a one way street. We are witnesses to it all the time. The wife who still loves her husband in spite of his contempt for her and his philandering. The prodigal son who, in spite of the loving concern of his parents, has only cold indifference for the ones who gave him life. This is love. Heroic loving. Who can deny it? But, as long as loving is a one-way street, it can never become a *love relationship!* It will always remain, "one-way loving."

If I am truly caught up in a love relationship, I will give and I expect a return on my investment. I know that does not sound very romantic. Nevertheless, it is true. I perceive my beloved not simply as the object of my love, but also as a source of love benefits. Consciously or not, I expect that my loving will trigger a positive response in my beloved and will cause her to love me even more. As long as I see our love relationship as strongly benefiting me, I will wish to pursue it. In the same vein, I realize that in order to bring about a favorable response, I must first increase my involvement in my beloved. I have to give so that she too will realize that I am good for her and I will be seen as a powerful source of her well-being.

When this happens, she too will respond and love me even more. By so doing, my perception of her as being good for me will once again increase and I will want to return her love (in order not to lose her) with more enthusiasm than ever. And, if all is well, the love cycle continues to grow in an ever-widening circle. Then, that love relationship becomes increasingly precious to both lovers.

If, for some reason or another, one of the lovers becomes discontented with the return on his emotional investment, then the trouble begins to surface. He holds back and no longer gives as freely nor as easily. He feels it is no longer worth his while the way it used to be. He perceives his loved one (rightly or wrongly) as giving him less than before. Unless something is done to reverse this downward shift, it is only a matter of time before there is no longer any desire on the part of one or the other, or both, to continue putting anything more into the relationship. Then, either one partner continues to love (one-way loving) or both of them recognize that there is really nothing left to their relationship and they separate.

The same is true of our relationship with God. We will love Him and respond to Him for only as long as we perceive Him to be a source of good for us. When we no longer believe this, then, you can be sure our love for Him will wane. There is a difference though. Unlike almost all of us who get tired of one-way loving, God goes on loving till our dying day. I suppose that is one of the most compelling reasons why He is God.

PERSONAL CHEMISTRY

WHEN THEY MET FOR the first time, they immediately liked each other. There was something in each of them that clicked. They felt good about each other without actually knowing why. It was just some kind of personal chemistry that coming together, caused both to draw closer.

There is more to personal chemistry than meets the eye. It is something mysterious. Something difficult to identify and almost impossible to explain. Why is it that certain people "hit it off" immediately? They need no long and complicated introductions. They do not engage in long and intimate communications. It is almost as though they have known each other a very long time. Their relationship becomes deep and intense in a relatively short period of time. There is a kind of mutual understanding that develops swiftly and effortlessly.

More than anything else, there is an acceptance of each other that is as admirable as it is rare. It is as though a natural liking for each other had automatically triggered a spontaneous mutual acceptance.

When lovers fall in love quickly and deeply, the personal chemistry factor is always present. There is a swiftness in the way the relationship is caused. The soaring level of concern and love is hard to explain. It all adds up so quickly that without the personal chemistry factor, the joy in the acceptance of each other would not be possible.

Just as personal chemistry promotes the growth of love, its absence is fatal to a relationship. Two very wonderful persons can meet and yet never be able to build a friendship because of the lack of personal chemistry. It seems as though, no matter how hard they work at fashioning a meaningful relationship, nothing works. They simply cannot "click" well together.

Sometimes, we run into people whom we instinctively dislike without knowing why. We admit to our inability to state reasons for our being "turned off." It is simply a gut feeling that we cannot explain. The personal chemistry does not mix well. In fact, it is as though the personal chemistry of one individual reacts adversely to the other and causes unpleasant side effects that nobody wants. Then there is a backing away, a desire to disengage from each other.

God has been good to us. Somehow, we all seem to run into at least a few people with whom our personal chemistry mixes well and quickly. These are the persons who mean so much to us and who have, over the years, become our loved ones.

Maybe, God created these combinations of personal chemistry in people so as to insure that even those unskilled in the art of loving would not be wanting in friends.

79

WHAT LOVE CAN AND CANNOT DO

THE EYE OF THE TYPHOON has just passed over us. The deceptive calm of the center of the storm has given way to terribly high winds and heavy rains. When the wind gusts, I can feel the house vibrating. It is as if the house is into convulsions.

For the past three hours everyone in the house has been manning "battle stations." Cleaning up the water that seeped into our home, removing hanging plants, and securing things that could be blown away. A window has just shattered. Out here in our subdivision, there are few homes and the winds come blowing across the open fields with an unobstructed fury. Our lights, telephone lines, and water connections have been knocked out.

The sky is dark. It is as if dusk is setting in on us. Yet, it is only mid-morning. The weather has deteriorated so badly that one wonders if the sun will ever shine again. But, we know it will. If we can hang on for a while, the winds will subside, the rains will cease, and the skies will clear. Right now, that might be difficult to believe. Just looking out over the stormy countryside, one could hardly imagine that this will ever stop. It will. Our faith and past experience tell us so.

In life, we also run into terrible storms. That is when everything seems to go wrong. A number of misfortunes befall us almost simultaneously. We get hurt and the suffering we bear is so intense that we feel it will never end. We are beset by a series or reverses and we wonder if things will ever go right for us again.

It is in times such as these that we need to keep our balance. In these difficult moments when it becomes so easy to give up that we need to man our "battle situations" and put up a good fight. Our faith in ourselves tells us that in time, if we do our part, our fortunes will change. We will witness the passing of the storm. After the high winds have subsided, there will be time for rebuilding, and perhaps rebuilding better than things were before the storm.

During the worst, we oftentimes find it is difficult to think positively. Because we cannot be sure about what the future will hold, we fall into the temptation of believing that the times ahead will bring more of the same.

We need to do battle with this kind of thinking. We must look ahead beyond the hard times. If we can do so, our spirits are lifted and we take heart anew. This new hope allows us to work hard to turn things around. And, more often than not, it is the extra effort that we exert that causes the turnaround.

MYTH OF PERMANENCE OF LOVE

WHENEVER TWO PEOPLE FALL in love (deep or superficial love), they experience an intense feeling of security. This security usually arises out of the feeling of permanence. Deep love, intense emotions, all imply permanence.

Ask a couple that is madly in love if they think it is POSSIBLE that their love may someday die, and you will find that amazingly few are willing to admit to the simple possibility of a break up. Most refuse to even think about it. In spite of the undeniable facts that surround us, most people in love will just not accept that there always exists the chance that their love could someday end up on the rocks.

There is this myth about the permanence of love. Oh yes, we know that love dies. In fact, we all are well acquainted with friends and relatives whose marriages have broken down. But, it is not possible for this to happen to US! Not US!

That is the myth. It can happen to others, but not to US. Our love is above all that. It is strong, healthy and so vibrant.

Right! But, even a healthy body today, can contract a disease next month. Even the strong can be undermined by factors that weaken and eventually kill.

Because most people accept the myth of the permanence of THEIR love as an absolute truth not to be debated or discussed, little is done in the way of CONSCIOUS preventive maintenance.

Love is like a car. It can be running very well now, but in the next moment, it can break down. Yet, some automobiles rarely break down because their owners are aware of the need for preventive maintenance. They keep checking their autos, even when they are running well. They fully understand that the nature of a machine is such that, unless it is carefully maintained, it will sooner or later fail.

Love is like that. I have seen too many healthy love relationships disintegrate to believe in the myth of permanence. By the way, I do not mean to say that permanence in love is impossible because reality has proven to us that it does exist. I am saying that love does not guarantee permanence, even if a loving couple feels that nothing can come between them except death.

I am a firm believer in preventive maintenance. Although I love my wife dearly and very deeply at this point in time, I also realize that, unless we both guard our love, we could lose it. If we are careless and take each other for granted; if we neglect the million little things that go into the making of a meaningful love; if we become sloppy, and our awareness level about each other drops to a low level; if this happens, then, I fully expect trouble.

I know that in maintaining an intense love, there is a certain degree of tension involved which flows from a constant vigilance. While guarding against a possible enemy, the sentries sense a certain amount of nervousness. Although confident of their abilities to deal with any intruder, they are aware that even the best fighter is useless, if he is asleep at his post. The best army is the one that maintains a sharp fighting edge, even in times of peace.

If your love is, at this moment, healthy and vibrant, thank God for it. You are at an advantage. Now, what remains is for you to guard what is so precious to you. If you don't, you might wake up one terrible morning and discover with dismay that your love is suddenly in trouble.

THE OPPORTUNIST'S LOVE

WHAT THE PSYCHOLOGIST said struck deeply into my heart. "When we ask someone the question: 'What have you done for me?' … We have ceased to love."

I thought long and hard about those words. Slowly, the full impact of what it meant made itself felt. And I had to admit that it was true.

How often have "lovers" used this same sentence to defend their arguments? How many times have husbands and wives thrown that question at each other? And what about teenagers who have been disappointed in love? Or individuals whose friendships have been frustrated?

The psychologist was right. The person who is looking only for his own fulfillment, or who decides to love just because he wants also to be loved will find that his efforts are all in vain. He will not succeed in establishing a true and deep love relationship because the focus of his attention remains on himself. That is where so many of us make a fatal mistake. We look at love and ask ourselves what we can get out of it instead of asking what we can give to further increase its intensity. In fact, most of us seem willing to GIVE only after we GET a little. We cannot seem to understand that we are looking at love in reverse. And perhaps this is the reason why it backfires on us so often. And perhaps that is also why we seem never to fully understand what love is all about.

We begin with the wrong premise. We start by focusing on ourselves when our attention and our concern should be centered on others. We see others as potential sources of self-gratification. We see others in the light of what they can do for us. And if we become convinced that they cannot make us happy, then we pick up our bags and walk away. In other words, if there is nothing in it for us, then we want to have nothing to do with love.

Because we become the starting point of it all, and we intend to be the end point, it is not surprising then if we fail in our efforts to develop a deep love relationship. As long as we are the "Alpha and the Omega," so to speak, we will surely fail in our attempts to be loved.

We will fail because we are pure and simple opportunists. And, although they may succeed in business, opportunists always lose in the game of love.

If we want to truly love and be loved, we must never use others as a means to our own ends. They must always be the end-object of love. We become matured only in as much as we are capable of shifting the focus of attention away from ourselves and onto others. We will become experts at loving only in as much as we have developed the ability to look away from ourselves and think of the well-being of others. Anything less than that will never do.

PLATONIC RELATIONSHIP

SOME WOULD HAVE THOUGHT her views to be strange. Others would have laughed and doubted her words. I took her seriously.

We were having a meal together with some friends. Somehow, the topic of conversation turned to men and love. She was still single, attractive, articulate and intelligent. She longed for a relationship, but just could not seem to get what she wanted. It soon became obvious why.

She had a serious sexual hang-up. She enjoyed the company of men … until they tried to touch her. She was happy with a "platonic" relationship. Whenever her boyfriend put his hand on her knee, she would get completely turned off and would lose all respect for him. The simple thought of going to bed with a man was totally repulsive to her. Especially seeing him naked. That was very disgusting to her.

Some of our friends smiled smiles of disbelief. Others said she was not normal. I could not be sure, but was willing to bet that she had been a victim of some kind of sexual trauma when she was still very young. I told her my suspicions and she admitted that it was so.

Bob Garon

It seems that when she was still a child, her uncle made her play with his penis. It was a terrible happening for her. It completely traumatized her and caused her to look upon the male organ with revulsion. Aside from that, there were strong feelings of guilt. She sensed it was wrong then and, later on, knew for a fact that what happened was immoral. That she was only a child and an obvious victim was not enough to offset the trauma.

This terrible experience, which is not at all uncommon in our society, had devastating effects on the woman and her views on men and sex. Sex for her is filthy. Never mind that it was ordained by God. Never mind that it is considered normal and natural. For her, it is the ultimate filth.

I explained to her that she was suffering from a strong sexual hang-up which, if not dealt with effectively, would have far-reaching negative consequences in any love relationship she would have. Unless she worked out her hang-up, she would make every man who approached her feel like the dirtiest person in the world. And this would surely drive men away. And if somehow, she marries with her sexual hang-up still intact, I predict loads of trouble. Since her sex life would have to be virtually non-existent, and the little that she did have would be traumatic, her marriage would have to be sex-free to suit her. If her husband felt the same way about sex and both could have a "platonic" relationship, then he and she could find happiness. If, on the other hand, her husband turns out to be like most men, then there will be no end to her marital troubles.

A MAJOR DECISION FACED BY A WOMAN

IT WAS THEIR SEVENTH date and she was beginning to like him a lot. He was a perfect gentleman who seemed genuinely caring about her. Their conversations were going beyond the superficial and were moving into the realm of the meaningful. She was a woman who had long ago been wanting a true relationship with a decent man. And now, he was there before her. At first sight, he seemed to be all she had dreamed of in a man. She was indeed a happy woman.

Then it happened. He made a pass at her. In fact, it was more than a pass. It was an outright invitation to sleep with him. At first, she was stunned. It was as if she could not believe him capable of such a thought. She did not know what to say. She surely did not feel like going to bed with him. The thought was revolting. What was more difficult to handle was the disappointment. It was almost as though she did not think him capable of suggesting such a thing.

At the same time, she felt flattered that he was attracted to her enough to want to sleep with her. However, this good feeling was more than offset by the dawning of doubts. Did he really love her or was he simply maneuvering to get her to bed? Was he sincere about the things he had said during prior dates? Or, was he simply setting her up? She was not a foolish and immature woman who knew nothing about life. She might have expected it had the relationship grown deeply and quickly. From another man, she would not have been surprised in the least.

When she turned him down he did not leave her. However, he did continue to bring up the subject again and again, as if to wear her down. After a while, their love grew and they became more serious about each other. The passes continued and one day she said yes to him. By that time, she believed that they would marry. Besides, her body longed for his too.

In the end, (nine months and many more sexual encounters later) their love broke up when he walked away. She felt terribly cheated. It was as if he looted her emotionally and physically. Bitterness set in. Much of her thinking and values had changed. She became more cynical about men, about life. The next time around, she told herself, things would be different.

When a decent woman goes to bed with a man (even if she loves him) she is making a major commitment of herself to him. As she does this, she is also compromising her moral values for the sake of the relationship. If it does not work out, as it oftentimes happens, the sense of loss is tremendous.

Before saying yes, a woman needs to think hard of the risks involved. In the same way, if a man truly loves a

woman, he too should give a lot of thought to what is
involved before making his advances.

92

SECRET LOVE

I RECEIVED A LETTER from a man (Chinese) who is madly in love with a Filipina. However, his is a secret love because his family wants him to marry a Chinese girl. He loves his Filipina and wants very much to marry her, but is worried about the reactions from his family and relatives.

He is interested in knowing what will be the repercussions if he goes ahead and pursues his love relationship. He also wonders if their future marriage will work well considering that they come from very different backgrounds and cultures.

This is a very difficult problem for me to comment on. Perhaps it is because there are so many dimensions to the problem. We need to look into how much the man's family means to him. Obviously, he will have difficulty with his parents. And they in turn, will surely make it hard on her in many ways. And, even if they marry against the wishes of his parents, if he is forced to live in his parents' house because of financial necessity, I think she is in for a lot of unhappiness.

If, on the other hand, the two of them have a measure of financial independence; if they can afford to live on their own without having to run to his parents for material help; then, one major obstacle will be removed. However, if his family is wealthy, he may have to run the risk of displeasing them, and getting financial help is cut off. If his love for his woman is enough motivation, then he will be willing to say goodbye to his material comfort.

Perhaps what will be most difficult to deal with is the possible rejection from his family, if he goes ahead and marries the woman of his choice. There is a strong feeling among some parents that their children have an obligation to follow ALL of their wishes and desires. So, it happens that parents order their children to undertake a career that they do not like. Regardless of the personal feelings of their kids, parents insist. And many children (most, in fact) follow only to give up their "forced careers" at a later date.

The same is true of love. Many parents have their own reasons for wanting a son or daughter to marry a particular person. Their reasons may clash with the desires of their children. It does not matter. Mama and Papa know best. And should the children refuse to follow, all hell breaks loose.

Unless a young person is willing to experience the anger and disappointment of his parents, he had better follow. However, if he is made to do something he does not believe in, then the price of his obedience will come high. Someday, when things go wrong and he is unhappy, he will blame them for his misfortunes.

If a young man feels he will need to displease; if he senses that he is strong enough to handle the resulting stress; if he believes he can fend for himself; if, ultimately love demands it; then, he should go ahead, marry his woman and be willing to face the consequences.

SEXUAL HANG-UP

EARLIER, I WROTE ABOUT a young woman who experienced sexual trauma while still a child when her uncle forced her to play with his penis. As a result of this terribly unpleasant happening, she grew up with a distorted outlook on sex and anything related to the male sexual organ. Any touch from a male would remind her of her experience and would turn her off completely. Although she was perfectly normal in every other way, when it concerned sex, she kept this hang-up which got into the way of a healthy male-female relationship.

Even if she kept her courtship with a man very clean, the more thought of any future possibility of having sex, (even in the context of marriage) would cause revulsion in her.

She was not aware of the fact that she was unconsciously searching for a man who would want a relationship without sex. Although a remote possibility, it was not probable that she would find such a man in her lifetime. And whenever she ran into a man that showed some normal, natural interest in sex, she was "disappointed" and would find ways to break off from him. What was a healthy relationship, suddenly became undesirable because of her sexual hang-up.

Of course, she kept bumping into men who were normal and interested in the sexual aspect of a relationship. Consequently, she was always asking herself "why are men like that?" What was a perfectly healthy attitude in males, she saw as some kind of perversion. And, because she had picked up this hang-up so early in life, she thought that HER view of sex was normal and the males she met were all messed up. And so, she went through life suffering because she could not find HER kind of man.

This woman needs help. She is in need of some therapy. She must find a therapist she trusts and whom she believes in. Then, she will have to spend long hours talking about what happened and discussing it until she is thoroughly convinced she was an innocent victim. Then, she may understand that her ongoing guilt feelings have no basis in truth, although they were born of a real happening. Much time will be needed to re-orient her views on sexuality. Otherwise, even if she finds a man and marries him, she will be condemned to a lifetime of inner conflict and tension with her man.

She will have to understand and accept the beauty of marital sex and what it can do to enhance a love relationship. She must learn to eventually enjoy sex with her husband. Failure to do so will almost certainly have adverse effects on her marriage. She must learn that sex in its proper context can be the cause of a greater growth in mutual love. If she somehow fails to gain these insights and change her attitude, there is practically no way that she can ever have a deep, meaningful love relationship with any man.

THOUGHTS OF DEATH AMONG LOVERS

THEY WERE BOTH MADLY in love with each other. Three years ago, they had fallen in love and ever since then, their feelings had grown progressively more intense. They were so happy, and yet, there were moments when they caught themselves talking about death. When they did this, there was a sadness that came over them that they found difficult to explain.

This is not an unusual happening among people who are deeply in love. In fact, they find themselves often thinking of death even if they do not talk about it because of the obvious unpleasantness of the subject.

I believe it was the philosopher Rollo May who wrote something about this phenomenon. He said that it is only when two people are very deeply in love do thoughts of death arise more frequently. The lovers feel so close to each other; they see themselves as inseparable. Somehow, they sense that it is only death that can come between them and destroy their relationship.

This it seems is the reason (at least one of them) for repeated thoughts of death among lovers.

When two people are intensely in love, there is such a strong bond between them that they feel a deep sense of security in having each other. They feel safe in their love. On the other hand, thoughts of separation, of losing each other, are more frequent because the lovers value what they have more than ever.

If you suddenly acquire a stock of diamonds, you begin to worry about thieves entering your house. Before you acquired this wealth, you did not need to be anxious because there really was nothing much of value in your house.

The man who owns an old, battered jeep does not even lock it at night because he feels confident that the rusty vehicle is worthless anyway.

In the same way, when there is little value placed on a relationship, the anxiety over losing it is minimal. If, on the other hand, a man has found an extraordinary woman and has built a deep and meaningful relationship with her, he necessarily will give more thought on how he might possibly lose her.

The moment thoughts about dying or losing your beloved to death become more frequent, do not be troubled. Just accept them as signs of the value you put on your relationship. Remain calm. Do not allow your feelings to sadden you.

There is only one thing you can do in such a case. Enjoy the "nowness" of the moment. Since you cannot avoid the reality of death, at least you can make the best out of the vibrant reality of life.

DO YOU WANT THIS AFFAIR?

ONCE I RECEIVED A letter from a reader that I would like to share with you.

Dear Mr. Garon:

My boss introduced me to a very charming fellow who is a perfect gentleman. He is not handsome or macho but he has the personality that a woman wants in a man. He wears his clothes neatly and he moves around with a lot of confidence.

He is friendly and generous and comes to the office every day to chat with us. He has taken us out for *meriendas* and lunch and has dated some of us. He makes us feel good and important, pretty and beautiful. Then suddenly, I sensed that he was paying more attention to me, and I got scared. I avoided him and he got the message. He was terribly hurt, and he never came back to the office.

I found out later that he was not getting along very well with his wife, and it was just a matter of time before they finally separate. I was also told that his wife is pretty but a person who is not easy to get along with. This man is very lonely, although he does not show it. He has sought friendship wherever and whenever he could find it. I feel very sorry for him, and this situation has bothered me. I like to befriend him again, but I am afraid that he might ignore me.

What can I do?

Very truly yours,

Name withheld

Are you sure you want to do anything? Remember, he is married and you are single. If you leave things the way they are, there will be no affair. If you pursue the matter and "befriend" him again, this could very possibly go further than simple friendship. Especially since he "is very lonely," as you say. Lonely men easily get themselves into affairs.

However, it is clear to me that you like him very much. Enough to write me about your feelings, and enough to want to initiate moves to rebuild your friendship. I assume that you are single... and lonely too. A lonely, unhappy married man and a lonely single girl: that's a perfect setup for an affair.

I have no doubt that you could have an affair with him if you desired. All you need to do is make the initial move. A telephone call to him asking him why he hasn't stopped by to visit the office will do. Chances are that he will take it from there.

The only question in my mind is this: do you really want this affair? I say "affair" because I doubt that you have a simple friendship in mind. You like him too. And

I believe that, deep in your heart, you long to have some kind of attachment to him.

Problem is that you may find yourself getting into something that is going to get very complicated. And, you may get hurt. On the other hand, you might find some degree of happiness.

So, it's all up to you. Think about it, and then decide to either proceed or hold back. And then, be prepared to live with the consequences.

THE INABILITY OF MANY TO LOVE DEEPLY

AFTER THE COUNTLESS contacts I have had with all kinds of people, I am deeply convinced that there are many persons who do not possess the ability to love in any way deeply. There are of course a number of complex reasons for this. Some of you may disagree with me vehemently, yet if you take a look around, you will no doubt understand what I am trying to say.

I am NOT saying that these people cannot love at all. What I mean is that they just do not seem to be able to ever cultivate a DEEP and MEANINGFUL love. Their loving can never seem to go below the surface. They remain superficial in their relationships and they cannot go beyond the first halting steps of friendship.

To get actively involved with an individual whose ability to love has been deeply curtailed is awfully risky. One can expect to give tremendously, and get very little in return. One can invest a great deal in terms of time and emotional involvement, and find himself trapped on a one-way street.

One sign of a person's inability to love deeply is the lack of many friends in his life. Of course, there are countless valid reasons for not having many friends. But there is nevertheless one solid reason why certain people do not have friends: they are just not very LOVING persons. To be loved, one must be lovable. And to be lovable, one must love. Not very many of us care to get emotionally involved in one-way deals. Most people who love expect to be loved in return.

The man who has few friends is usually very critical. He easily finds fault with people. He quickly discovers what's wrong with people. This knowledge prevents him from seeing what's right with them. He ordinarily will keep himself at a distance and tends to remain uninvolved. He may suddenly give all his attention to one person and it appears that this may be the only person in the world he loves. That could be true. However, I would not bet on it.

He who has a great ability to love cares for lots of people in an authentic and sincere manner. He does not reserve all his loving for one individual. Unless there are circumstances beyond his control, the man with few friends is in such a situation because he rarely practices loving to any significant degree.

Another sign of the inability to love is excessive ambition. The man whose only reason for being is to acquire millions of dollars has little time for anything else. Don't expect him to make great long-term emotional investments in love. They distract too much from his primary purpose of living.

Bob Garon

Ambition can exist in countless fields and is a good thing. However, when it becomes excessive, then you can be pretty sure that loving people takes a back seat.

"RUDE AWAKENING" IN LOVE

SHE NEVER BELIEVED that she could end up so disappointed over anyone. In fact, she wondered how she could have been so wrong about a man. In the very beginning, it had been love at first sight for both of them. She was a woman who loved intensely. And so, when she loved, she really loved. She gave her all without any kind of reservation. All along, she thought he was doing the same.

She was wrong. Her friends told her so. They said she was purposely blinding herself so that she would not see the terrible truth. She denied anything of the sort. Yet, her friends were right. He did not love her as intensely as she loved him. More than that, he was, all the while, falling out of love with her. At first, he would not admit it. Then, one day, he said so. They parted ways. She was heartbroken because the separation was not of her doing and she wanted no part of it. But, what could she do? She had no choice because he insisted on saying goodbye.

She told everyone who would listen that he had changed. She said, she no longer recognized him. She wondered why he had become so different.

Bob Garon

The fact was that he had not changed. He was pretty much the same as when she had first met him. Oh yes, there had been some degree of evolution in his personality and character. However, there were no basic changes as she claimed.

What happened was that she had painted her own idealized picture of him since the very start. Glossing over some apparent weaknesses, she made him out to be someone he was not. She did this little trick in her mind. She created the man she wanted to have. Then, she fit him into her thinking so that she saw him as her dream man. When she looked at him, she did not see him as he really was. Instead, by refusing to look at certain realities about him, she was able to maintain her view of him that she had created.

Of course, the whole thing was a charade. But it was make-believe that she could carry on as long as she could suppress the realities she was trying to avoid. And, she did this by running away from the issues that were being raised. She ran and ran and ran, until she could run no more. That was when the unpleasant truths about him surfaced, and she could no longer avoid them or deny them.

After the breakup, she said he had changed. Not true. He was the same as before. The difference lay in her discovery of his true self. He had never changed. She had changed him in her mind. He had not tried to deceive her. She has done her own self-deception. It was only her own "rude awakening" to the facts that she could no longer ignore that caused her to finally see the truth about him.

We are all guilty of bending some aspects of reality in our minds. We do this only half-consciously or in a totally unknowing manner. We do it because it serves our purposes. However, we do it for a price. And the price can be high. Reality always has its day. And when that time comes, it can be a terrible awakening.

WHEN LOVE TURNS SOUR

WHEN LOVERS BREAK UP, things can never be the same between them again. More than that, things will almost surely be worse than before they fell deeply into love.

Take May and Ed, for example. They met at work and, before long, Ed was asking her out to the movies. Then there were dinners in the restaurants and dinners at home, where she got to know his parents. It was only a short while later when Eddie asked her to go steady with him. She was overjoyed. And their love grew quickly from that time on.

Then, one day, she learned that he was seeing another woman on the side. There was the inevitable confrontation, the resulting arguments and the breakup. May was angry. Angry at herself for having loved him so, and given so much to their relationship. She also felt cheated. Such poor returns for such a heavy investment of herself. Insulted by his disloyalty, she was embarrassed by the whole experience.

He felt mortified by it all. He really liked May more than anyone else. And, he regretted having put his fingers into other pies. He never thought she would walk out on him. And now, he had to face her every day at work. And since their work caused them to interact daily, it was tough going. There was a great deal of tension between them. They both wished they could have transferred to other departments, but that was not possible.

After a few months of this kind of stress, May decided to resign from the company and looked for work elsewhere, far from him. It was all too much for her to handle and she had enough.

Whenever you fall in love with someone, please remember that if the relationship does not work out, the chances of a smooth break and a pleasant aftermath are extremely slim. Most likely the break is going to be painful and the relationship afterwards (if there is anything left to it) can be expected to remain very strained indeed.

Perhaps this is inevitable because of the very nature of loving. There is such a high level of expectations. And when these are dashed to the ground, you can imagine how disappointed the lovers can be. Aside from this, love always calls for a great deal of giving.

However, no matter what lovers say about giving and expecting nothing in return, the truth remains that every lover DOES expect a great deal in return. And, when this does not come, one feels cheated and taken for granted. The resultant anger is in direct proportion to the level of disappointment one may feel after perceiving that the relationship will never work out.

Under these conditions, it is just about impossible to expect that it will be "business as usual" between lovers, after they say their bitter and angry "goodbyes." It is a seeming paradox that two people who cared so much for each other when they were in love, can care so little now that it is over.

TIRED OF LOVING

SHE STILL LOVED HIM, but the stresses and tensions on their love were building quickly. He was a good man. However, he was in a steep dive. Things had gone wrong for him. He had lost his job and could not seem to find any kind of meaningful work. He turned to drinking in his moments of desperation and this only worsened the situation. He simply became a more difficult man to live with. Through it all, he seemed to forget his wife and three children.

Falling into a kind of lethargy, he could not seem to shake himself loose from the depression that enveloped him. It wasn't as though he had given up trying. He made efforts to pick himself up, but they were only half-hearted and produced negative results.

During all this time, the wife stood strong. Continuously encouraging him, she always had kind words for him. She reassured him at every turn. She showed him lots of love and affection. However, all her efforts seemed to amount to nothing. On the contrary, the situation continued to deteriorate.

After a while, when things did not improve, she found herself weakening in her love for him. She was getting tired. Tired of always giving and getting nothing in return. Tired of having him lean on her and not being able to lean on him once in a while. Tired of listening to his problems while having no one to turn to with hers. Tired of carrying the family alone. Tired of doing all the loving and not getting any love in return. Tired of always being tired.

After a while, she could no longer bear it. The burden was too heavy. One day, she asked him for a temporary separation.

When giving is lopsided; when it is constantly one way; when there is little or no return on one's emotional investment; then, you can be sure that the resulting tensions will take their toll on a relationship. When two people consent to mutual love, both parties know that the loving will be uneven. Today, one gives more. Tomorrow, the other carries the heavier load.

Although this is expected and even welcomed, it is so only up to a point. When one finds herself giving everything and getting little in return, then the whole relationship is put into question. Going on and on in an endless giving pattern without expecting anything in return, can wear down the resolve of even the strongest lover. Time will come when continued loving will lose its appeal. When this happens, the end is near.

WHEN DREAMS BEGIN TO UNRAVEL AND FALL APART

SHE LOVED HIM WITH a love that was deep and sincere. There was admiration and respect for the sterling qualities she found in him. For many years, it seemed, she had waited for this kind of man. And now, it looked like things were going her way.

He responded to her love with a show of affection that swept her off her feet. Kind and thoughtful, he simply made her feel like a queen. The time they spent together never seemed to be enough. They were in love and the greatest enemy of lovers, is the clock that signals the end of another loving experience.

As the months passed, they talked of marriage. She was elated. Visions of a home and children and years of marital bliss filled her head. Her dreams were becoming a happy reality. As she began to prepare herself for the big day, she noticed a change come over him. It was difficult to define, because it was a subtle change. Perhaps it was more a feeling of discomfort on his part.

At first, she paid little attention to it. She simply shrugged it off as the pre-marital jitters. However, there came a point in time when she began to share his discomfort. She just could not get him to agree to a date to marry. He kept putting it off with a host of reasons that she suspected were excuses. She became impatient and pushy. He resisted and showed his displeasure. Soon, the tensions between them began to rise. They were into an escalating war of words until finally, he called the whole thing off.

She had strong suspicions that perhaps he had no intention to push through with the marriage in the first place. Chances are she was right. The fact is that many men want to have their cake and eat it too. They will promise their women everything under God's blue heaven. However, when it comes time to deliver on their promises, they seem to have short memories. That is when dreams begin to unravel and fall apart. This is also the time when hearts begin to crack under the strain of unfulfilled expectations.

It is important to understand that there are those who find it difficult, and oftentimes impossible, to make a serious commitment to another person. There are men for whom a lifelong commitment is unimaginable. They simply relish their freedom too much. Getting tied down is an ugly thought that they would rather not deal with.

However, they fully understand that most women will frown on an intimate relationship that has no chance of producing a firm commitment. For this reason, they resort to all kinds of promises that they do not intend to keep. They lead on their women and motivate them to carry on with them by dangling before them hopes and expectations that are false to begin with.

BREAKING UP AN AFFAIR

IT WAS A VERY LONG letter from a young lady in deep trouble. Briefly, she fell in love with an older man who relentlessly pursued her. She was innocent, naive and a virgin. He was smooth, knowledgeable and a good talker.

Before long, he talked her into bed. Full of guilt feelings, she wanted to break off the affair, for she was a good woman. Yet, she was a jumble of feelings and somehow the affair went on. Then, one day she learned that he was married with three children.

She confronted him. At first, he denied it. Then, he admitted it was true. He begged her not to leave him. He told her he loved her. He no longer loved his wife. And, if she were only patient for a while, he would separate from his family and they would make their lives together, just the two of them. Time passed and his words remained empty promises.

Now, she wants to get out again. Trouble is, she says she does not know how. She is not even sure if she truly wants to leave him. He took her virginity and that might be a factor for hanging on. (I think it is.) She is asking me what to do.

It is difficult to say. It all depends on what it is she wants. If she desires to break off, then that is what she should do. Break. There is no easy way. She needs to simply say goodbye, ignore his pleadings and his tears, refuse to be swayed by her feelings (and his) and walk off into the sunset.

Of course, all this is easier said than done. There will be hurt. There will be fear and loneliness. There will be anxiety and apprehension about the future.

Yet, what choices does she have? It is a lousy situation. The chances of his leaving his family are almost zero. If anything, I think he is simply leading the girl on. He has no intention of making his life with her. To go on is to prolong the agony. To postpone the breakup, is to make it that much harder in the end.

The problem is that she is so full of feelings that they are getting in the way of her decision-making. Her feelings are making so much noise that she cannot hear herself think. She is confused. Like a shocked child standing in the middle of the ruins of a house, she is unable to move.

Let us be honest. She has feelings for him. He did not put a gun to her head and force her into bed. She went with him time and time again. It was not just his fault. It takes two to tango. She said yes, even if it was a reluctant yes. She agreed to carry on, even after she learned that he was married.

Now, she is the prisoner of a lot of heavy emotions and she cannot seem to break out of. She is a hostage to the happenings that she willfully helped bring about. She is trapped in circumstances that are just as much of her own making as his.

Granted that she was an innocent babe in the woods. Granted that he took advantage of her, and quick-talked her into the affair. And granted, she was no match for him, still, she had, and still has, the ability to walk away.

If she does not do so, it is because she prefers not to. No matter how strongly her conscience tells her to leave him, she somehow feels that there are also some positive trade-offs that she stands to gain if she carries on. Perhaps, she is still hoping against hope that he will make good his promises and leave his wife. Maybe she values the excitement of the affair; of being pursued; of being "loved." Whatever the motives, as long as it is unclear to her that her affair will lead her nowhere, she will find it difficult to break it up.

The moment she is convinced that the negatives far outweigh the positives, then she will quickly do what she has been hesitating to do all this time. Until then, more pain, more agony.

LISTEN TO WHAT PEOPLE DON'T SAY

JOHN POWELL, A PSYCHOLOGIST, once wrote: "To understand people, I must try to hear what they are not saying, and what they perhaps will never be able to say."

Loud protestations to the contrary, the cold fact remains that we are not really very honest and open to others about our feelings and ultimately about ourselves. We spend much of our working hours fooling others and ourselves.

The older we get, the more adept we become at throwing up smoke screens and faking out people who are seemingly getting too close to us for our own emotional comfort. We learn to act as if everything is fine when it isn't; to smile at an enemy when we feel like smashing a vase over his head; to say "I love you" to the wife when there is only intense hatred in one's heart.

Then there are moments when people are unknowingly dishonest with themselves. The reason for lying to themselves is usually quite simple. They need to protect themselves from some very harsh truths about themselves.

A woman vehemently denies that she is, because she cannot face the fact that she is insecure in her marriage.

Bob Garon

A young girl emphatically stated that she hates boys. She fails to understand that the reason for her excessive hostility to males is the sad experience of having been attacked by a man when she was still a child.

An estranged man beats his children regularly, and says he does not know why. The deep truth of the matter is that his kids remind him of his wife, and he beats them because he is subconsciously taking revenge on his wife.

There are lots of feelings (good, bad, and indifferent) buried within the deepest recesses of our troubled hearts. They stay down there, far below the surface, because we do not know how to handle them. We play it safe and keep them hidden, rather than bring them out in the open and have to deal with them and be uncertain of the results.

For this reason (and others too), it is very important that we listen to what people don't say when they engage us in any sort of meaningful exchange. People send signals that come up from the subconscious a little bit like the criminal who does his best not to get caught. A girl who cuts her wrists a little and talks about killing herself, is really asking for attention. The talk of suicide is only her way of shaking people up enough, for them to sit up and take notice of her.

In love, friendship, or just plain getting along with people, it is vitally important to listen to what people don't say. Only then, can we begin to fully understand what makes people tick.

ONE-WAY GIVING DOESN'T PROMOTE HEALTHY LOVE

THE GREAT ABRAHAM LINCOLN once gave his formula for being loved.

"When I want a man to love me" he said, "I ask him to do something for me."

This recipe is quite different from what most people believe. More often than not, we think that by doing things for people, they will understand how much we care and they will love us. Not true.

There are legions of spoiled children whose parents have done everything for THEM; who have hardly needed to lift a finger for their parents; who have been given things right and left; and who, in the end, have bitten the hands that fed them. When the giving is a one way kind of giving, then you can be sure that this kind of process cannot give birth to a healthy kind of love. Perhaps, the reason for this is that love of its very nature demands that there be giving on both sides. One-way giving creates a distortion of love that is oftentimes very misleading.

The mother who is doing all for her son, while he does nothing for her, may think that they have a beautiful love relationship. The truth of the matter is, that no such love exists between them. She, no doubt loves him, but strong indications of his love for her are sorely lacking.

I have often wondered, what comes first: love or doing things for someone. I used to believe that you loved first and then did things for your beloved. Now, I think the reverse is true. It is the "doing" for someone that gives birth to love. There may be attraction and infatuation which cause us to want to do things for someone. However, it is only after we have committed ourselves to some kind of act that is beneficial to the other that real love begins to grow.

This no doubt that explains a mother's love for her child. She has done so much for him since his birth, that she almost has no choice but to love him.

It is difficult to love a man who will not allow you to do things for him. Think of it! He refuses your gifts, turns down your invitation to dinner, etc. He wants to do things for you but won't let you do him favors. I say you will not love this man. You may benefit from his kindness, but you will not love him.

Until he allows you to do something for him, he is engaged in one-way giving which does nothing to promote healthy love.

WAITING FOR ONE'S LOVE

SHE WAS A WONDERFUL woman. Pretty, attractive, intelligent, and genuine. She was also 26 and single. And, that worried her. She wondered if she would ever get her man. Over the years, she had longed for a relationship that would be meaningful and deep. But somehow, it never materialized. In fact, she began to wonder if there was something wrong with her, something basically wrong with her personality. She was not sure. Meanwhile, she waited, and waited, and waited, and waited some more.

Perhaps, waiting was part of the whole problem. When I talked to her, she told me that she was waiting for her man to come into her life, but it just wasn't happening. I believed her. She looked like a woman who was waiting for something, someone. In fact, the way I saw it there was something about the WAY she waited that somehow turned men away.

It was as if she sat there waiting for someone to make things happen. It was as if she was unwilling to do anything for herself to HELP make things happen. It was as if any man who approached would get little or no help from her.

I said it was "as if". I am sure, that had a man approached her she would have been overjoyed and thrilled. Yet, I am not at all sure that she would do much to push her relationship forward. I think the man would have to do double-time. I believe she would play pretty hard to get.

The danger there is clear. It is altogether possible that the man would be unwilling to undertake such a one-sided task. She seemed to be the type who would not be very eager to give. This was not clearly stated, but there remained a kind of unspoken undercurrent that seemed to indicate this. I think this is why men stayed away. To convince another person that it would be a good thing for him to begin investing in a relationship, there needs to be indicators that it is so.

Eugene Kennedy had a few insightful lines on the subject:

"The greatest myth about friendship is that it will come to people without their doing something in exchange for it. That is, people believe that others will respond to them automatically. They have a feeling of entitlement to affection and friendship. They seem to say, 'Payment is due to me.' That is a terrific handicap because friendship is a dynamic relationship in which we must yield something of ourselves before we can get anything back from others."

She did not give the impression that she was willing to give to others. One felt that she was eager enough to receive, but that there would be no guarantee that she would engage in the same level of giving.

Before we approach a person to extend a hand in friendship, we expect to see signs that our investment will show some returns. When the signs of it being so are few or non-existent, we hesitate, then go somewhere else in search of a potential friend.

WHEN WOMEN CHASE MEN

ONE OF THE MOST PITIFUL sights that I see during my counselling is the single girl who is chasing after the man who got her pregnant, in order to force him to marry her. It is a tragic scene to witness. The woman is in a state of emotional panic. She wonders about how people will condemn her and whisper about her, if they find out that she is with a child. There seems to be no way out for her. It is either marriage, abortion or disgrace.

Abortion is distasteful. It runs against the ethics of most women. It also goes counter to the natural instinct that every woman possesses. Her body was designed to carry, nurture and give birth to a child. Besides, babies are beautiful, loving. Most of all, they are one's own flesh and blood. That is why so many women decide against abortion.

What then, about the disgrace, the social stigma that is associated with the unwed mother? The prospect of having to face the cold stares of friends and relatives; having to wonder if she will be accepted as a friend by strangers she is just getting to know; thinking about how she will explain her child to the next man she loves; calculating the chances of his breaking off with her after he finds about her indiscretion; all this, and so much more causes her to shudder at the thought of society, friends and relatives "finding out."

She then is left with only two more options; have her child and face the world, or marry. Even if it isn't going to be a good marriage, countless women choose a relationship which they know will not be happy. Even if the man does not love her and even if she hardly loves him, the pregnant woman would still rather marry. After all, there are so many unhappy marriages. Even if the chances of a future separation are high, a broken marriage is better than being an unwed mother. Separated women are very numerous, and count among them well-known personalities. One is less noticed in such company.

So the chase begins. The nervous young man at first tries to avoid the woman he so thoroughly enjoyed not so very long ago. He was imprudent in his search for pleasure, and now, they say that he must pay dearly for his escapade. Perhaps the price will be a lifetime of unhappy living with someone he no longer loves.

In the end, after trying hard to avoid marriage for which he is totally unprepared, he finally capitulates and settles down with the woman he will now begin to resent because she forced him into a situation he tried hard to avoid. One can be pushed into a marriage of convenience, but one cannot be threatened into love.

How can we as a people help to do away with this kind of situation? What can we do to make it easier for such women to avoid compounding their mistakes?

Bob Garon

We can be more understanding. We do not have to encourage premarital sex, but we can help young women to stand up again, after getting hurt in a fall. We can, by not playing God, stay away from making moral judgements on people. It's really none of our business what happened. Besides, the Lord can take good care of the situation without any coaching from us.

Tenderness, love, understanding, that is what is needed. Then, we have a whole lot less unhappy marriages.

LOVE THAT COMES AND GOES

SOMETIMES SHE FELT SHE loved him so much. He could be such a nice man. Polite and sensitive, there were moments when she could feel herself being swept off her feet by him. He somehow made her feel so secure and so safe. And, so loved.

Yet, there were times when she thought she wanted to leave him. He showed deep selfishness. He remained insensitive to her needs and her feelings. During these moments, she disliked him intensely.

The problem was that her feelings of love seemed to come and go. Sometimes, she saw him as the greatest man in the world. Then, she was convinced that he was the biggest bum she had ever met.

These "stop-and-go" feelings constitute what is called "ambivalence." Ambivalence is the experience of simultaneously having positive and negative feelings toward an object, person or situation, of being pulled in opposite directions psychologically.

We may have ambivalent feelings toward someone for a long time. It is as if we cannot make up our minds about whether or not to like him. Since neither the positive or negative feelings can seem to stand out strongly, there is a kind of emotional "swaying" that is going on.

Ambivalent feelings may last as long as a lifetime. Unless and until either the positive or the negative far outweighs the other, the ambivalence will remain. The moment I become very positive (or very negative) about a person, the ambivalence disappears. Then, I either like or dislike an individual. My feelings are no longer in doubt.

Ambivalence can create a lot of stress and tension in a person. The emotional pulling and pushing that is going on can cause an individual to be torn. Ambivalence is a kind of emotional conflict, a kind of emotional war that is going on inside. And, it is always difficult to maintain peace and serenity in the midst of such conflicting feelings.

Perhaps the most common feelings of ambivalence are felt towards parents. Especially when it concerns teenagers. Teenagers are in a period of transition from the dependence and the protectiveness of the family to independence and self-reliance. They resent the rules and regulations laid down by parents. They want to be free, yet they cannot exercise the degree of freedom they desire. They wish to be on their own, but they cannot afford it.

So they resent their parents. Sometimes, they feel they hate them. There is stress and tension in the family as the teenager maneuvers and manipulates, and the parents counter his moves with some actions of their own.

On the other hand, he loves his parents. He understands that in spite of everything, in spite of their restrictions, nobody loves him more than his Mom and Dad. And his love for them is preventing him from hating them outright. And so, his feelings remain ambivalent, a jumble of the positive and the negative.

Later on, as he matures and grows into adulthood; as the rules and regulations are gradually lifted; as he understands and appreciates his parents more, the positive feelings overwhelm the negative. Then the ambivalent feelings, the emotional conflict and stress all disappear.

FADING MEMORY

FOR MANY YEARS, SHE had exercised the greatest patience. Hoping that things would work themselves out. Praying that some kind of miracle would happen. However, the same situation remained static over the years. And now, she had given up hope that ANYTHING would ever happen.

What had always been, was still, and she believed would forever be. During all these years of waiting for him to get his act together, one thing though HAD changed. Her love for him had fallen off to a point where it was just a fading memory. She had lost all respect for him. And since respect is an almost exact barometer of the level of love, it was safe to say that she no longer loved him. Yet, she had remained in the same house with him over the years.

There were a number of reasons for this. Her children. She wanted to keep her family together, even if "togetherness" meant constant conflict and personal pain. She was convinced that a loosely held family is better than no family. Others disagreed with her, but that was her thinking and she ordered her life accordingly.

She also did not delight in the prospect of being the talk of her social circle. She was truly embarrassed about the thought of separation. Perhaps it was because she believed people would see her as a failure. Besides, she was frankly a lonely woman even under the present unhappy circumstances. Imagine what it would be like if she went off and lived alone.

However, perhaps the most persuasive reason for not leaving him was that she had loved him for so long. It had been genuine love. And deep too. But, as the years passed and the hurt accumulated and eventually eroded her respect for him, her reasons for hanging in there became less convincing.

Then, one day, she awoke, got out of bed and decided that this was the time to say goodbye. He, of course, was stunned. Why? She tried to explain, but he would not understand. Perhaps it was because she had lived with the situation for so long without making any move.

Why only now? He could not understand the slow but steady process of erosion that had taken place. He had been confident that such a thing would never happen. He had always believed that she would never dare do such a thing no matter how unhappy she might be.

He was wrong. She did leave. She moved into the house of her son who welcomed her with loving arms. The children? They not only understood, they told her that they wondered why she had not made her move long ago.

They could see her pain and her suffering. They knew she was unhappy and their hearts went out to her. They realized that what had been happening over the years was terribly unfair.

And her friends. Her real friends totally supported her. She found refuge in their consoling words and their caring.

Most of all, she discovered that it was not all that difficult. In fact, a short while after her exit from her marriage, there came a strange peace over her. What she feared would be a terrible experience, actually became for her a kind of healing process.

BROKEN COURTSHIPS

YOU HAVE OFTEN HEARD it said that one must be careful of the rejected woman. However, the spurned male is no pushover either. There are men who cannot accept a "no" answer from a woman. It is as if a negative reply constitutes an insult of the greatest magnitude.

When a man courts a woman, he must understand that the very nature of courtship contains the possibility of failure. After all, courtship is a tryout, a period of time that is allotted by two persons to get to know each other. In no way, does it imply commitment. In no way does it suppose an obligation to carry on the relationship or to allow it to develop into something permanent.

On the contrary, the nature of courtship allows for a quick separation if needs be. It makes it easy to get out of a relationship if one or both persons feel that, for any reason whatsoever, going on is no longer in their interests. In other words, the rules of courtship were established precisely to facilitate an "easy-getting-in-and-easy-getting-out" type of relationship.

For these reasons, nobody should get overly upset about a broken courtship. If they play it by the rules, that is. However, not everybody follows the rules. There are all kinds of bending of the rules and the writing of new ones that is going on.

Take sexual intercourse, for example. In our society, sexual intercourse is seen as something pretty serious. Two lovers who go to bed are saying something to each other. Theirs is more than a simple kind of courtship. It now gets more complex. At least, for the woman.

Women in this country (except for prostitutes), do not generally indulge in sexual intercourse "just for kicks." Sex means more to them than vulnerable pleasure. It means a kind of commitment, a giving of oneself with the hope of promoting a deeper, and more meaningful, more permanent relationship. I doubt if many women would consent to going to bed with a man tonight if they knew he would be gone tomorrow morning. And so, it is always difficult to get out of a courtship that has creeped into bed. Such a relationship hardly ever breaks up without a lot of anger and bitterness.

Another kind of courtship that is difficult to say goodbye to is the one that has taken on the flavor of commitment. When all sorts of plans and promises of marriage have been made, expectations rise. And when expectations go unfulfilled, there is always unhappiness and disappointment. The deeper the involvement, the greater the expectations of marriage, the harder it is to say farewell and the longer it takes to forget.

When two people get into courtship, they would do well to establish, as much as possible, ground rules and limits. And, they should make it very clear that either one of them can say goodbye at any time.

And, when it is over, let it be all over. Let bygones be bygones. Let the parting be friendly. Let the good times form a gallery of fond memories. If it is at all possible to have a friendly break-up, then all efforts should be made to cause that to happen.

If, however, this is impossible because of the anger and the hurt, then it is in the best interest of everyone concerned to break off all contact for some time. Harassment, looking back, feeling sorry and guilty are all useless exercises that only sap one's emotional and psychological strength. When the end comes, let it be the end.

WHEN A RELATIONSHIP ENDS

A MARRIED WOMAN WHOSE husband left her for another woman came to me one day for counselling. She told me that she had every intention of making him pay for leaving her, by making life miserable for him. She wanted to punish him. After all, he was guilty of breaking up their marriage and family life.

I told her that I believed that her plans to retaliate were a bad idea. And I told her why. There had already been a whole lot of hurt. The conflicts they had been into before he left the house had caused deep and gaping wounds on both of them. They had suffered terribly. Now, just when the war was all over, she intended to resume hostilities. The hurting of each other would start all over again.

What was the point of it all? Why start fighting again? When a battle is lost, the general who cares at all for his men will retreat and try to save as many as possible from certain destruction.

It's amazing how some men and women who have been frustrated and rejected in love act. Instead of admitting that they have lost and that it's all over, they carry on a useless fight which only serves to further damage both parties.

There is enough destruction that takes place when two individuals who were once in love separate. Both feel cheated. They believe they have wasted time, energy and commitment in a useless exercise. When a good businessman realizes he has an operation that is losing money and cannot be turned around, he gets rid of it or closes it down. He then goes on trying to recoup his losses in some other endeavor.

When a love relationship has not worked out; when it has soured and has proven to be a poor emotional investment; if it is beyond repair, then, it is time to behave wisely and get out and not look back.

Let's face it! Both parties lost out. Does it really matter if the man ends up with another woman? Even if we put a gun to his head and force him back, it would all amount to nothing. Resorting to dirty tricks will only cause the vindictive one to waste precious time and energy on somebody he no longer respects.

Instead of getting into this exercise in futility, she would do better picking up the pieces of her shattered relationship, and should look more positively into the future.

The vengeful person who goes out of her way to get back at her estranged husband is like a mental patient who is banging his head against a stone wall. The wall still stands and he is bleeding in the head. The woman who seeks revenge and succeeds in making life miserable for her former husband is only hurting herself. While striking out at him, she is building up in her heart a level of viciousness that will spill over into her other relationships.

You cannot hate a man without the echoes of your hatred being heard in your interaction with others. Neither can you hate and behave in such a destructive manner without this negative experience influencing your future behavior. Some people who get into a "hate trip" have difficulty getting out of it. Your ability to love is diminished every time you hate.

If a loved one walks away and there's nothing you can do about it, **CALL IT A DAY!** Don't force reality into your own mold. Accept it for what it is. Surely, you will love to live again… if that's what you want.

Instead of looking back on a disaster, look ahead to the bright new dawn on the horizon. The rest is history.

UNDERSTANDING WHAT MAKES LOVE TICK

THERE ARE ALL KINDS of strange mysteries in relationships of love and friendship. There are so many things that happen when people fall in love which are difficult to understand.

The other day, Emmy was telling me this. She was saying that she cannot understand all the factors that came into play and caused us to love, to marry, and to feel the closeness that we now experience. There are so many unanswered questions. More than that, there are even more unasked questions. Unasked because we do not have the necessary insights to be able to formulate them.

How is it, for example, that of all the women I have met, it was Emmy I ended up loving and marrying? What was the combination of circumstances that caused our paths to cross? What was it that made us "click" as a couple? Why the peace and harmony we now experience?

The answers to these and countless other questions are so complex that a lifetime is not enough to find answers. There are so many underlying factors that are impossible to discover because they are so complicated and so deeply buried within us. And yet, we go on loving without really understanding all the whys.

Bob Garon

Writers through the years have used much ink and paper trying to explain things about love (I have joined them) all without too much success. Nevertheless, there is a constant effort to somehow find out what makes love what it is. There is an impulsive desire (it is almost an obsession with some) to get to the bottom of the make-up of love.

Perhaps it is because we sense that if only we can know all about loving, we can better make use of our knowledge to cultivate the kind of relationship we have all dreamt about, but which has proven to be so elusive. And there is much truth to this, I think. The more one understands what it is that brings two people together and keeps them together, the more chances the individual has to build himself a more solid love.

I am absolutely sure that my long experience as a marriage counsellor, has greatly contributed to the avoidance of many of the mistakes I have seen made by my counselees. And, because of the privileged position I have as one whom people confide in, I have witnessed the beauty in so many relationships. I have been able to learn some of the secrets that constitute a meaningful love. This, I have used in my own life, my marriage and in the way I am trying to educate my daughters, Vanessa Anne and Maria Alexandra.

I strongly believe that the deeper your understanding of what makes love tick, the stronger will be your chances of success at loving. Even if you are aware you will never be capable of knowing all the secrets of love, the more your understanding, the greater your chances of happiness.

What is of utmost urgency is the desire not to give up looking for answers. More than that, there must be a strong motivation to search for the right questions.

LOVE IS A GREAT RATIONALIZER

THERE ARE EXCEPTIONAL INSTANCES in which a person, due to mental illness, undergoes a radical personality change after marriage which could not be foreseen. Aside from such exceptional cases, a person's basic personality is firmly fixed by the time he or she comes to marriageable age. In a courtship of any reasonable length of time, one's basic personality can be recognized by the other party, if he or she has open eyes.

Unfortunately, love (or physical infatuation) is a great eye closer and a great rationalizer. "I know he drinks a little," (he is tipsy on half of their dates), but that's just because he is so shy; he'll be alright once we're married." "Sure she's kind of bossy, but she's such a sweet kid, you don't mind that; and once we're married I'll wear the pants." "He does fly into a temper tantrum over such little things and it seems that we're always quarreling; but he's nervous and high strung. Marriage will change that." "Gosh she's jealous! I can hardly kiss my own sister. But I suppose she's afraid she might lose me; after we're married, she'll be different."

We all have heard wishful thinking such as these. Sometimes it is because physical desire has put reason to sleep. Sometimes it is because the defender is so anxious to get married that he or she will settle for almost any kind of partner who comes along.

Then too, there are the pathological cases: the mother-dominated son who unconsciously seeks a wife who will dominate him; the girl who is driven by unrecognized guilt feelings to choose a brutal husband who will provide the punishment she unconsciously craves.

Original sin has disturbed the control that reason should exert over the biological urge, so it is perhaps not too surprising that many young men and women walk blindly into a marriage doomed to unhappiness; they walk into it in spite of the danger signals that are flying at full mast for any intelligent person to see. The alcoholic husbands, the nagging wives, the vicious-tempered men, and the insanely jealous women; they suddenly didn't develop their undesirable traits after marriage. And the naive belief that "I can get him (or her) to change," flies in the face of all the psychological evidence, the evidence that a person's basic personality pattern does not change after maturity.

A person may grow in virtue with the years, but deep seated emotional and psychological disorders usually will grow worse, barring a miracle, of course, and few miracles of this kind occur.

Fortunately, those who see marriage as a vocation (and thank God they are a legion) do retain some vestiges of discrimination and do try to make a wise and prayerful choice.

However, even in the great multitude of normally happy marriages, there are sometimes areas of stress which arise from the mistaken idea that another person can change his personality at his or her command. An important ingredient of happiness in marriage is the willingness to accept each other "as we are." The perfect match is a rare phenomenon. Almost inevitably, there will be personality differences and clashes of temperament. The need is to adjust to these differences, rather than expect to change them.

If a wife is by nature a poor manager, no amount of griping is going to make her a smart budgeter and an efficient housekeeper. It will be a happier marriage if the husband will accept and love her as she is, and quietly do his best to make up for her deficiencies (as she almost certainly is making up for his.)

If a husband is by nature a quiet stay-at-home type of person, no amount of complaining is going to change him into a party-going crowd-loving individual. A vivacious wife may find this a trial, but it will be a happier marriage if she cheerfully accepts the fact, and stops trying to make the man over.

The wife may be an inordinately neat individual who can't stand the sight of a pin out of place, and her husband, a sloppy fellow who never puts things away. The man may be an obsessively punctual person who wants everything done on the dot, and the wife a flighty person who never has dinner ready on time.

"You have your faults and I have mine. Let's just accept each other as we are. Let's be willing to settle for the good that we find in each other (and look for the good) so that under God, ours may be a happier home." That is a simple and yet infallible philosophy upon which to build a day-by-day satisfying marriage.

Blessed will be the children who grow up in the peace and the charity of such a home.

SMARTNESS OF LOVE

LOVING IS NOT JUST fun; it's a smart thing to do. That may sound like a crazy opening sentence, but I mean it.

Everybody admits that loving is the primary need of all human beings. There is no doubt about that. Yet we are not consistent. Oh yes, to love a dear wife and an affectionate sweetheart is natural and very easy, and we do it all the time.

What about our enemies and those people who get on our nerves? Do we love them too? Yes, but that's different. It may not be so easy. And even if it were, why should we? Because Jesus told us to do so. Perhaps he didn't realize what He is asking us to do. It isn't natural to love one's enemy.

Nobody said it was the natural thing to do in the first place. But it is the smart thing to do. Let me explain.

When you have an enemy you hate intensely, you wish him bad luck. Now be honest and admit the truth. You don't really wish him God's choicest blessings, do you? Though it's embarrassing, let's face it. We are often tempted to pray that an enemy falls down the stairs and breaks a leg. We often experience a sick kind of sadistic satisfaction in watching an enemy sink miserably to the floor and bleed.

It isn't right, and we feel guilty about it. Perhaps that is why we are not more vocal about our negative feelings.

Whenever we hate an enemy, we generally are sorely disappointed. Why? Because it is so hard to watch an enemy rise and be successful. If the person we hate so intensely is happy and satisfied, his happy state increases our own frustration and uneasiness. It can be painful to watch an enemy climb the ladder of success higher and higher. An enemy who is a big success in life is a thorn in our side.

If you love deeply and truly, you share in the good fortune and the pain of your friend. You hope for his success and pray that he rises if he falls. That's the way it should be.

It's smart to love because it's miserable to hate. To refuse to hate is to refuse to be unhappy.

DYNAMIC RELATIONSHIP

I WAS JUST REFLECTING on what it takes to keep a dynamic relationship exciting. To me, there is a need to have excitement in a relationship. Otherwise, boredom sets in, followed by trouble. Seems to me that the very nature of a love relationship calls for excitement.

The problem is that we easily get bored and tired of things. Like little children who, after a while, walk away from the most expensive, sophisticated and mechanically complex toys. We get so high at the beginning of a relationship. So excited. It is as if this is the best thing that has ever happened to us. Then, a few months later, the relationship sours and comes to an end.

It is as though we cannot seem to maintain the momentum in a relationship. It seems like we begin to fade quickly. It is as though we do not know what to do next to keep things going. It is like we cannot shake off the boredom that is coming over the relationship like a dark cloud. It is as though we have run out of technology to maintain the enthusiasm that is beginning to die.

In some relationships, it takes a long time before this point of oncoming boredom is reached. In others, the glitter of the early days is quickly lost. And in other cases, after years of friendship, years of marriage, it is still there as vibrant as ever.

Those relationships that have lost the excitement and enthusiasm of the past may still be intact. However, they have lost their shine and polish. The couple seems tired, and though they stand together, the dynamism is gone. And both people secretly long for those past days when they could get excited over each other.

Not that it is necessary to have all kinds of movement and a multitude of activities. Quite the contrary. Long-lasting dynamic relationships have a kind of serenity about them, a kind of peaceful quality that radiates. Like old friends of 30 years who still enjoy playing cards together 3 times a week. There is something there that holds them together; something that causes them to truly enjoy each other. They are not married; they are not bound by any official commitment. Yet, their relationship is vibrant and vital. It is alive and breathing. There is strength to it that is difficult to explain. There is a vitality to their friendship. From whence it comes, remains a mystery of sorts.

I myself have seen this radiance in a relationship many times. I have also searched for it in vain, in many others. Where it was present, I always found that love was alive and well. Where it was absent, I found a relationship in trouble, a love that was sick, or the remains of a love that once was.

What couples can do to guard and cultivate this excitement in order to make it grow, is not easy to explain. I suppose every couple needs to work out their own formula. However, what is important to understand is that, if you feel you are losing that sense of excitement about your beloved and can admit it (or if you've already lost it), then your relationship is in trouble, even if you are not arguing and in conflict.

If you have it (that feeling of excitement), don't worry about your love. It is alive and well.

BE LOVABLE

LOVE IS THE KEY to happiness. We all know that. What is less clear to most people is that in order to be loved, one must be lovable.

When the orientation of a man's life is centered on himself and the satisfaction of his own needs, he is self-centered. When he goes out among his peers and exploits them and manipulates them in order to gain some form of acceptance and love, he is self-centered. When he can think only of himself and neglects the well-being of others, he is self-centered.

We may pity him, feel for him, and try to help him, but the fact remains that he is self-centered. And being self-centered, he is not at all lovable. He is concentrated on himself. And for as long as things are thus, he will remain self-centered and unlovable.

He should not then be surprised, if he remains unlovable. He should expect to be alone and unwanted most of the time. And surely, his maturity and emotional growth will be stunted. He will forever remain an emotional child.

If, however, a man learns to go out of himself, turn himself away from his self-interests and in a generous way involve himself in the lives of others with a sincere desire to do them good… this man will most surely be loved.

A psychologist put it very clearly: "If a person seeks not to receive love, but rather to give it, he will become lovable and he will most certainly be loved in the end.

This is the unmistakable law under which we live: concern for ourselves and convergence upon the self can only isolate one's self and induce an even deeper and more torturous loneliness.

It is a vicious and terrible cycle that closes in on us when loneliness, seeking to be relieved through the love of others, only increases.

The only way we can break this cycle, formed by our lusting ego, is to stop being concerned with ourselves and to begin to be concerned with others."

This, of course, is a lot easier said than done. Even the most generous and the strongest men find it difficult to turn the focus away from ourselves and onto others.

This usually calls for a lifetime of continuous effort at training oneself to be people oriented; it means fighting against the inner forces that cry for satisfaction; it calls for a noble spirit that men must mold.

This strength of character and firmness of conviction comes about only after long years of persistent efforts.

In other words, in order to get used to being good and kind to others, there is only one way: **practice.**

THE DATING GAME

One of the most common points of conflict in any home where there are young people, is the dating game. Every parent fully realizes that the day will come when a guy gets interested in a girl and vice versa. There's no denying this.

The question is always when and how. When should a young girl be allowed to have a boyfriend? When should she be given permission to go to parties? How often should a youngster be allowed to go partying? How long should a teenager stay out at night?

I have witnessed some very violent arguments that stemmed from disagreements concerning dating and parties. And resolving such a conflict is not an easy matter because there is so much involved.

Everybody is aware of the importance that young adults attach to socializing. Interest in the opposite sex is as strong as it is strange during the teen years. Parties are important because they are points of contact. Young adults can meet new friends and hopefully find a sweetheart. And at this age sweethearts are top priority.

When teens don't get a crack at parties, they not only feel left out, they also see excellent chances for making friends slip through their fingers. It's a little like being an outcast.

On the other hand, parents worry about their children. They realize that they are young, immature, and inexperienced. It's not so much that they don't trust their children; it's just that they don't trust the people their kids go around with. Parents have heard about parties that degenerated into orgies and pot sessions. Although the percentage of parties that turn out this way is very small, parents tend to exaggerate their number.

Parents are also stricter with their girls. Why? They fear the loss of virginity. When a girl is late in coming home, mom and dad are thinking of the worst.

The kids enjoy parties so much that they hate to leave once the music and the dancing begins. What makes everything more difficult is that parties don't start at 7:00 P.M. anymore the way they used to.

Another factor that is hardly ever pointed out is that expectation plays a vital role in teenage parties. Half of the fun is in talking about an up-and-coming party and getting ready for it. Girls spend countless hours discussing what to wear, who's dating who, etc. That's also why teenagers usually brood longer than usual, when it concerns requests for parties that were denied.

Whenever parents seek my advice about these matters, I always point to the most important factor: Maturity. I'm not referring to physical maturity. In fact, a young girl with the body of a woman is in greater danger, if her emotional development has not kept up with her physical growth.

Parents must know their children. They must be sharp enough to see when their youngsters are ready for dating and partying. Then they must carefully judge how much freedom they should give. All these is not easy for parents to do because they have their prejudices and personal feelings to consider as well as objective reality. And what is most frightening is the thought that, too much restriction will make their youngsters negative, and that not enough supervision could mean tragedy.

DETECTING A CHEATER

THE YOUNG WOMAN SAT slumped in her chair, tears running down her cheeks. She told me she had discovered that her boyfriend of one year had married another woman. What hurt her most was that he had not told her about the marriage. She had learned about it through friends. When confronted, he said that it was she that he loved, and that he had merely been forced to marry the other woman.

How often have I heard that same old story? How often have I listened to that same lie about being forced to marry, but not really loving the wife?

Listen, ladies, the line about being forced to marry her but "really and truly" loving you, is perhaps the oldest and most commonly spoken lie used by married men when they attempt to court simple women. And I do not understand why women cannot see through this obvious falsehood.

Firstly, forced marriages are usually caused by pre-marital sex and pregnancy. The guy went to bed with the woman, and then, pressure was put on him to marry her. If this is so, then, either he loved her when they slept together, or he lied to her about loving her. Unless a woman is a prostitute, she will not ordinarily want to sleep with a man she feels does not love her. So, if he slept with her and did not love her, what makes you think he cannot do the same to you? Every day, countless men sleep with women they do not love. It is not a rare happening. On the contrary, it is common.

Then why does the man say such things? Simple. He has to convince you that he is sincere; that he is not cheating; that you are his "one and only." What do you expect him to tell you? That he wants to have an affair with you? He knows you are decent. And he also understands that you do not want to sleep with him if you know that he still loves his wife. If you can be convinced that he loves you and only you, then, getting involved becomes easier because it is more rational. Going to bed with a man you are convinced does not love you, but only wants to enjoy you sexually, makes a little sense to you because you are only being used. And who likes to be used?

Remember that the man who loudly protests that he loves you, and not his wife, can easily be put to the test. Ask him to leave his wife and live with you. He most likely will ask for time. Then, tell him he can have all the time he likes, but no sexual contact until he makes up his mind. Then, see what happens. Chances are that he will walk away and look for an easier target. And, when he does, do not feel bad about it. You have saved yourself from a lot of heartaches.

Bob Garon

Most men will not leave their wives. They simply want to have their fun and still keep a "good standing" in the community.

In other words, they want to "have their cake and eat it too." If you allow it, then chances are, you will become just another "piece of cake."

THE POWERFUL, FORMIDABLE "WEAKLING"

A MAN DOES NOT HAVE to be big to be strong; and a woman need not be tiny to be weak. Very often, a weakness can be turned into a winning formula in this complex game of life.

Women, who are supposed to be of the weaker sex, use many techniques to gain superiority over the stronger sex. A woman is usually bargaining from an inferior position, in terms of brute strength. And she knows it too. She understands this so well, that she has learned to make the most of her drawback, and uses it to get a lot of leverage in any conflict she is engaged in with a man.

This is what I call, "The Power of Tears." That is, weeping and crying. Women know that tears contain chemicals that can, among other things, melt a man's heart and transform the bitterness in his attitude into a sweet disposition. She has learned this from her youth, and has used her knowledge to an advantage. How many men have said: "Alright, we'll do it your way," or "Stop crying, if that's what you want, it is okay by me?"

When a man sees a woman cry, he tends to think that some catastrophe of major proportions has come upon him. Because tears do not come easily on or off at will, by most females. Ever since the beginning of time, women have used "The Power of Tears." to their great advantage.

Another technique a woman uses in order to get what she wants is nagging. By constantly repeating the same request over and over again, she can drive a man to give in to her desire, by forcing him into submission. A man who is the unfortunate victim of an expert nagger, will do just about anything to get even one moment of peace. How many big men have gone down silently to infamous defeat at the hands of a "little nagger?"

Another method that a woman uses to get what she wants is ridicule. By laughing at him (and there are countless subtle ways of laughing AT A MAN), a woman hits him at his weakest point: his vanity. She can just about destroy a man by continuously knocking him down.

Every time she brings him to his knees by laughing at him, she is wounding his vanity. Man is extremely sensitive at this point, and more than one has been completely crushed in this way by a "little woman."

Another method a woman uses to get her way, is the use of indecision. She refuses to come to a decision that is clearly hers to make. The man, in complete exasperation, then keeps fishing around for something that will please her. In the end, he will suggest what she wanted in the first place, and she will then agree to it. But she is making it come from him.

Perhaps one of a woman's most powerful weapon is her refusal to give herself sexually to her mate. She knows she is sexually attractive. She is fully aware of a man's intense sexual drive, and she uses her physical attributes expertly not only to entice him, but also to keep him in line by threatening to withhold her sexual participation. Countless husbands have come to know this through painful frustration, and by being sexually deprived of their mate's body.

Because these are strong measures, they often backfire and explode in a woman's face. She has gone too far and her efforts have proved to be self-defeating more than once.

Regardless, a woman has shown herself to be a powerful and formidable "weakling."

THE BLIND LOVE

IT IS AMAZING HOW open we can be about some issues, and so closed about others.

I remember a young couple. They were unofficially engaged. "Unofficially," because although neither one of them admitted that they were going to marry, their whole pattern of behavior indicated otherwise. They courted intensely. Their lives became synchronized as they tried to do everything together.

There were, however, some very thorny issues that neither one of them cared to face. Their characters and personalities clashed on a number of points. Although they did their best not to offend each other, there were moments when they simply could not avoid conflict because their true selves rose to the surface. Yet, they refused to draw any conclusions from these difficult moments.

Their values systems were different too. Of course, they shared some values because it was this common sharing that kept them together. They were somehow able to avoid discussing some very vital issues that would have surely brought conflict into their relationship.

Ordinarily, these two individuals were well-balanced in their thinking. In these issues concerning some sensitive matters about their relationship, there was a kind of block. Not only would they avoid confronting the consequences of these attitudes, they would altogether refuse to discuss the future of their relationship.

Why? Why would mature, thinking grownups suddenly be so blind to existing realties? Why would they even refuse to talk about their implications? The answer can be found in fear. Fear that an honest and frank review of their relationship will cause them to see its inevitable negative results, and finally indicate to them that a breakup is the next logical step.

It is amazing how dreamy we can be when we really want something. We block reality out of our minds. We look the other way, even when it taps us on the shoulder. And when finally there is no way out, but to discuss the issues without hesitation, we deny reality.

The couple above would not face some glaring issues about their love, because they felt so threatened. They truly feared that the logic of it all would call for them to say goodbye. Even if the whole world could see that the relationship could not possibly work out, and told them so, they would not listen.

Perhaps, it is because of situations like this, that those who came ahead of us coined the expression: "Love is blind." In fact, it is not really blind. If anything, it is unwilling to see. It puts its hands up in front of its face and walks forward. If it stumbles and falls down, it is not because of its "blindness" but because it refuses to see.

What is sad is the fact that so many couples are heading for the edge of the precipice. Friends are shouting warnings to them. Because they are both of one mind in their determination to marry; because they have played games and tampered with their logic; because they do not wish to see; because of all these, they moved ahead, oblivious to the danger. And when disaster strikes; when the relationship explodes; then, they are "surprised."

They need not be. They refused to see the signs. They blocked out the warning sounds. They manipulated their thought process. And when all was said and done, they harvested what they planted.

SHATTERED LOVE RELATIONSHIP

THERE IS A LINE in a song popular some time back. It expresses perhaps the most fervent wishes of lovers, especially newly married couples. It goes something like this: "You're mine, all mine, now and forever."

When two people fall in love, deeply in love, they get that certain feeling of security. They think themselves to be so very fortunate to have been brought together by coincidence or by force of circumstance. While in the midst of experiencing all the intense emotions that are the ingredients of true love, lovers feel that their love is indestructible and will last till their dying days.

Well, things are just not so. With love, reality is harsh and hard. The truth of the matter is that countless love relationships are shattered everyday all over the world. There are no statistics to bear me out, but I believe every minute of the day sees at least one couple breaking up and separating for good. Every hour sees courtships spinning out of control, friendships going sour, and marriages crashing onto the rocks.

This is a cold raw reality which can hardly be denied. As a result, disappointments, heartaches, and heartbreaks abound. I'm sure that if you are sensitive, and care enough to look around, you can easily see many people whose dreams and expectations in love have been shattered. And you will find people whose hearts have been broken more than once because of a love that failed to work out.

Perhaps one of the reasons people are emotionally brought to their knees by unsuccessful love relationships is that far too many think that, once they have found their true loves, things must last forever. Maybe it's because they refuse to accept the very real possibility of a breakup. Consequently, they don't guard their love with the vigilance that it demands. They get careless and overconfident. And before long, although things are going out of control, they don't accept the reality of what's happening. Then everything simply explodes, and the parties involved wonder what happened.

Love is a delicate plant. It needs twenty-four-hours-a-day care. And unless it is carefully guarded, it dies a terrible painful death.

SCRIPT WRITING IN LOVE

WHEN PEOPLE FALL IN LOVE, they usually have visions of the kind of happiness that awaits them in the future. They see themselves enjoying each other, doing things together and possibly getting married, having children and "living happily ever after."

Lovers have all kinds of expectations of love. Oftentimes, these expectations are unrealistic. A woman has always imagined her lover to be sensitive and highly communicative. She has dreamed of having a man who could sit with her and talk with her for hours. However, the man she fell in love with, is the quiet type, who prefers to watch TV rather than chat.

She is very disappointed because of this. She constantly tries to get him to talk. Much as he loves her, conversation does not come easily. He is just not the talkative type.

She gets terribly frustrated with his "inability to communicate." The reason for her frustration though, is more because of her unfulfilled expectation. More because she had always wanted a man who can talk, and she had almost written a script in her head which she expected him to follow.

Bob Garon

All of us write out scripts when we love. We have some very well determined ideas about what we expect from our beloved in terms of behavior, attitudes and values. And, when the beloved does not live up to our expectations, we are disappointed and saddened.

The problem with some of our scripts is that, they do not suit the character, thinking and the personality of the beloved. It would be difficult for Burt Reynolds to play the part of a ballet dancer. No matter how wonderful the script, he would not be very convincing.

The same is true of the script lovers write for each other. They are often inappropriate, insensitive and out of character. And, the lovers fail miserably to play the part.

What is important in love and courtship is to do the casting carefully. It is vital to know the person well, before committing to a relationship. That way, one can be reasonably sure, that the script and the character, will come together properly.

Finding the right person to fit your script (your expectations) is no easy matter, however it is absolutely necessary if your expectations are to be fulfilled.

GOODBYE TO LOVE

PERHAPS, THE MOST DIFFICULT part of an affair is ending it. Whenever two people get involved emotionally, intellectually and sexually, the price of saying goodbye will necessarily be high. Maybe, it is because the involvement is so great, especially when both parties went into the relationship sincerely and with open eyes.

Nobody who falls in love, wants the love and affection that he invests in, the emotion that he experiences, and the degree of commitment that he pledges to come to nothing. Unless a man is playing games and has no intention of pursuing a love relationship seriously, his involvement with a woman means much to him. He would have to be insane to inject so much of himself, of his time and of his effort if he were not well-meaning.

All the goodwill, the growing expectations, the expanding hopes for an exciting tomorrow; all these things put together make a powerful recipe for loving. And, when it all seems to sour, to die; when the expectations are dashed to the ground; when deep involvement seems to come to nothing; when the whole affair begins to collapse, there is something that makes it difficult for us to believe that soon it will all be over.

Perhaps, it is because we do not wish to accept the fact that we made the wrong decision in the first place. Perhaps, it is the "shame" of having to accept "failure." Or, maybe it is simply that we feel cheated.

After all that has happened, we are left empty-handed. And, we feel so foolish and bitter. This is perhaps why so few couples can break up and still remain friends. The wounds are too deep, the hurt and disappointment too intense, to permit any kind of friendship to go on. What is left is a desert. And friendship must surely die in such a hostile environment.

And, maybe that is how things need to be. Very few of us are so noble, so calm in the midst of such an emotional tragedy, that we can say goodbye to love, and carry on in friendship. Very few can deal with smashed hopes, painful disappointments and a sense of betrayal. Very few can forget. The memories and the scars are such, that it becomes a necessity to bury the past, and the reminders of that past.

Whatever you agree is the truth contained above, it should be enough to make us pause for long moments, before committing ourselves to any kind of serious involvement. It should also cause us to be aware of the distinct possibility that a proposed love may not work out. In fact, there is a very real possibility that it could cause a whole lot more pain than we can ever suspect. The history of mankind is full of countless incidents that have proven this to be true. To think that it could not happen to us is naive and immature.

Before getting involved with another human being, we would do well to think hard about the possible unpleasantness, as well as the advantages involved. By doing so, we protect ourselves against unrealistic expectations. And, if we think things over well enough, there is a chance that we may even decide not to get involved at all.

LOVERS LOOK IN THE SAME DIRECTION

A THINKING WOMAN who was very much in love once wrote some beautiful lines: "I believe in this: That people who love each other are people who do not spend their time looking at each other, but are people who look in the same direction. I also believe that WORK is LOVE made visible."

When I first read this thought, I was struck by the simplicity of expression and the truth contained therein. It's true. Lovers DO look in the same direction. They may not see things in the same way, but for a love relationship to survive, it is absolutely necessary for there to be at least a general meeting of hearts and minds.

Some of the happiest couples I have ever met were people whose visions and ideas were similar in many ways. When things are not so, then you can expect tension and stress to come into the picture. The behavior of individuals is influenced by their directions in life. When two roads start crossing, there are mix-ups, traffic jams and mashups.

I guess all of the above can be summarized in one word: Incompatibility. Incompatible individuals are those whose directions in life inevitably clash and create friction and uneasiness. People who "cannot get along with each other" are those tragic figures whose visions are located in opposite directions, and who just cannot see both sides at a glance. And the direction in which they are forever looking, is not usually that of the loved one. Hence, there is the inevitable difference of opinion because the vision is altogether different.

No matter how much two people want to love, they are doomed for failure, unless they get their visions and dreams somehow tied into each other. The success of their relationship depends on the degree of "getting their thinking together." Once they do that effectively, the inevitable differences will be easily resolved.

Although people are all unique individuals, there must be a commonness of viewpoint to some extent, at least if there is to be a deep, lasting friendship.

NO CARING WITHOUT LOVING

TO CARE IS A SIGN of authentic love and concern. When my friend says he cares for me and I can feel his care, then I know he loves me. If he says he loves me, and I feel he does not at all care for me, then I believe he is a liar and a manipulator.

Perhaps he DOES care for me, but unless I can FEEL that he does, it is as if his caring went for nothing.

The word "care" finds its root in the Gothic word "*kara*," which means lament. The basic meaning of care is: to grieve, to experience sorrow, to cry out with. This is not the usual meaning we give to the word. We tend to look at caring as an attitude of the strong toward the weak, of the powerful towards the powerless, of those who are fortunate enough to have towards those unfortunates who have not.

THE TRUTH of the matter is that, we very often do not feel comfortable about entering into one's suffering, and sharing the pain he is experiencing. In fact, the people closest to us and who mean the most are those who have shared our deep sufferings and have agonized with us.

They need not be those who gave us good pieces of advice when we needed them. In fact, advice given without feeling is often most offensive and usually ends up rejected, even if it is exactly what is necessary.

It is the one who FEELS for us that we appreciate. It is the man whom we FEEL understands us (because he shares in the pain we experience) who gets through to us and is most effective. He need not really say anything. It is enough that we know he feels what we feel.

THE REASON why some learned preachers are not listened to, is because the people cannot, as the teenagers say, "feel them." The people do not sense that they are on the same wavelength even though the preachers seem to have all the right answers.

It is most difficult to "care" for someone who has just lost a loved one. He is confused, disoriented and often finds himself doubting the goodness of God. When he asks the usual "why," it is easy to give him all kinds of "good counsel."

It is more painful to put an arm around him, tell him "I don't know why" and simply stand there in silence and share the emotional and spiritual pain he feels.

TO CARE, then, means to be present to each other. Just being there when you are needed is what counts. We have a strong tendency to run away from painful realities or to desperately try to change them as soon as possible.

But cure without care makes us into controllers, manipulators and cold counsellors. This is the kind of cure people would rather do without. This is why people so often refuse help and reject sympathy that is given in a patronizing way.

Bob Garon

In the end, I guess it all boils down to real loving. There can be no caring without honest-to-goodness loving.

LOVING SOMEONE WITH CHILDREN

SHE LOVED HIM DEEPLY. He knew she was the woman for him the day he set eyes on her. From the start, theirs was a beautiful relationship. They had much in common. And they complimented each other.

Since the death of his wife years ago, he had suffered through much unhappiness. There was the trauma of her unexpected and swift passing away followed by a difficult period of grieving. The loneliness that he had to live with was exceedingly burdensome. What carried him through it all was his love for his three children. He had been father and mother to them. And they responded to his love in kind. They were closer to him now, than ever before, and their loyalty to him bordered on fanaticism. And that was the problem.

Although he was in love with his woman, and wanted very much to take her as his wife, the children (now teenagers) were strongly opposed to the idea. In fact, he had oftentimes confronted them for their less than polite attitude in her presence. And yet, he did not wish to force the issue too much for fear of further aggravating matters.

She tried hard to accept his children and be accepted by them. It was not easy. She could sense heavy resistance coming from them whenever she held out her hand in friendship. As they refused her love, it became more and more difficult to go back and try again, and she found them less and less lovable.

Yet, she knew that unless she won them over, she would almost surely lose him. Loving him meant loving them too. There was no way he would choose her, if he was given an ultimatum. His love and devotion to them was overwhelming. And he was a principled man whose sense of duty would not be sacrificed, even for love. He knew it. She knew it. And, the kids knew it.

The wooing of the youngsters took much time and caused her stress and tension. Loving him and building her relationship with him was a whole lot easier than dealing with them. He realized this and tried to help as much as he could. After many months, the complicated process began to pay off. Slowly, almost painfully, the youngsters went from tolerating her, to liking her, to accepting her somewhat, to finally loving her.

Loving someone with children is always a complex matter since it involves so many people, all of whom have their own self-interests to protect. The problems arise when these self-interests clash, as they inevitably do. The kids resent the would-be stepmother because they see her as replacing their mother, to whom they owe undying allegiance and devotion. They see her as a threat. She could distract their father from them and end up getting more of his love and affection than they. Their father might even leave them for her in spite of his promises to the contrary.

The father finds himself walking a thin line indeed. He has personal needs that the children cannot possibly meet. He sees the woman doing that. Yet, his love for his children cannot be denied. He cannot leave them. So, he is forced to bring all the parties concerned together in harmony. Not an easy thing to do. And yet, failure to do so could jeopardize his love for his woman, his relationship with his children, or both.

COMPETITION IN LOVE KILLS

RICARDO HAS A VERY beautiful and talented wife. She works in a bank and has risen to a position of responsibility in a comparatively short time. But on the other hand, he is a simple clerk in a commercial establishment, and there doesn't seem to be much chance of his going very far because of his limited talents.

This situation irritates Ricardo to no end. He secretly resents his wife's success and has been trying his best to convince her to quit her job and stay at home. His wife has fought this suggestion all along for financial reasons. The whole situation has created lots of bad blood and endless conflicts.

What Ricardo refuses to see is the fact that subconsciously he is jealous of his wife, and feels that she is wounding his ego by outshining him. The wife, on the other hand, is also asserting her superiority over her husband.

What is, in fact, going on is a stiff competition between husband and wife. This is a very unhealthy situation and if left uncorrected it will surely ruin what might have otherwise been a fine marriage.

Once competition steps into a marriage or a love relationship, many things begin to go wrong. The competition often grows quite fierce, and the competitors pull out all the stops, in order to come out on top. This includes the use of all kinds of emotional dirty tricks.

The husband will reach into his bag of knowledge about his wife, and search for any weaknesses he can find. He then usually proceeds to use this emotionally lethal weapon against the woman he loves. It's really unfair. Emotional warfare between two people in love can be a very rough, no-holds-barred affair.

People in love should understand that competition between husband and wife is most destructive and can only bring about lots of pain.

Love is a sharing in which two people rejoice in the joys and successes of each other. The happiness of one is readily shared with the loved one and vice-versa. Whatever benefits one benefits the other, too.

Competition in love kills; sharing gives life.

DISALLOWED IN MARRIAGE

SHE WAS SIXTEEN, PRETTY, with a sweet personality. She was also very nervous as she sat in my office playing with a tissue paper. Her Mom and Dad had a troubled and puzzled look about them which one could sense only slightly covered deep inner pain and frustration.

The parents had come to see me because their daughter had run off with her boyfriend, a youngster of the same age. They had just returned from the province and faced their respective parents with an accomplished fact. They had been to bed together and they now wanted their parents' blessing on their planned marriage.

The girl's parents had other ideas about the whole affair. For one thing, they didn't like the boy. He was a "long-haired hippie type" and a dropout, who couldn't support himself and whose future looked bleak indeed.

The boy's family was more than willing to get the two married off to each other. The girl's parents worried about their eagerness since they felt that, because of their superior economic position, the guy's family might simply be looking for material gain from the union.

Upon questioning the young lady, it soon became crystal-clear that she really knew nothing about the duties and responsibilities that she would soon be forced to assume if the wedding went through. Surely she loved the boy. However, her love was not the kind of mature love that makes marriages click.

Love has many degrees of intensity. One may love enough to continue a courtship, but not enough to marry. Another may love enough to marry, but not enough to keep a marriage together for more than a few years.

The young people have their own ways of forcing their parents' hand. Most often, they run off and sleep together. They know that shame will force their parents to give in and allow the marriage in order to save face.

What they don't realize is that in doing so, parents most often condemn their children to a life of misery and marital hell. The youngsters' first mistake is compounded by their parents' "thoughtlessness." I used the word "thoughtlessness" because that's exactly what it is.

It's not premarital sexual intercourse that makes for a solid foundation for marriage. And the loss of virginity doesn't make things better either. Add emotional confusion and immaturity, and you have a number of very good reasons NOT to allow a marriage.

Besides, the shame of the family can only be greater in the long run, when the couple eventually break up. Most likely, by then, there will even be children to think about.

When one thinks about it, one wonders why parents are willing to risk the future happiness of their children on an almost sure losing proposition. I suppose selfishness and a sense of self-protection have a lot to do with it. It's hard to accept, but it's the truth.

LIVING IN A WORLD WITHOUT LOVE

IT IS AMAZING HOW cold the world we live in is. We often hear people talk about how impersonal and how uncaring we are towards one another.

Because of this, we sometimes get the feeling that we are living in a world without love. Maybe this is the reason for the alienation that we feel around us. Young people sense this. That is why they resort to drugs, drinking and unbridled sex. They are searching for meaningful relationships. However, since their search is fruitless, they invariably turn to distractions which are in truth escapes from the reality of a loveless world.

Perhaps you are willing to try a little experiment that will drive my point home. Take a few moments and think about the names of those people in your life who really and truly care for you in a deep and meaningful way. Now, I am not talking about those casual "friends" you may have. I am referring to those people who REALLY care for you with a concern that is strong and constant. If it is convenient for you, write down their names.

Chances are that you will come up with only a handful of people. If so, don't feel too bad because ordinarily the people I have asked to do this average only about five or six names.

Whenever people perform this little exercise in awareness, they are suddenly overwhelmed by the fact that so few people really care. In a world of more than four billion people, it comes as a rude shock to suddenly realize that perhaps only four, six, eight, or maybe ten people really care for you. One suddenly feels very much alone and alienated.

After this little experiment, you may get a feeling of loneliness even in a crowded room. Chances are that you may also begin to wonder if you are lovable. You may perhaps even get the feeling that you are exceptionally unloved.

Please don't feel that way because things are just not so. The fact is that all of us are lonely. Even those happily married couples feel lonely at times. We all suffer from "love deficiency." Every one of us is in need of a healthy dose of love and deep concern.

I remember a line from the movie "Charly." Charly asked his teacher: "Ma'am, how much is too much love?" The teacher looked at him and smiled: "Just a little bit more than anyone can give."

If we feel we are not loved enough, it is because we are not loving enough. It is an indisputable fact that those who give most love receive the most love. It is also true beyond the shadow of any doubt that those who give little concern receive even less in return.

The problem is that we are all standing around waiting for others to love us. We fail to comprehend that the key to being loved is the willingness and the ability to go out and love others first. When people feel that we care, they respond in kind. When they can sense that we are waiting for them to make the first move, they get scared because they fear that we will ask too much from them, and give them too little in return.

I suppose the lesson to be learned from this is quite simple. If you want to be loved, go out and love.

THE TRAGEDY OF ONE-WAY LOVE

ONE OF THE SADDEST happenings to behold is the man who refuses to take "no" from a woman, and continues to pursue her, even when the message is clear that she doesn't love him. Perhaps the only sadder thing, is the sight of a woman running after a man who gets irritated by her mere presence.

What makes these scenes so tragic is that they clearly violate even the most obvious reality. The insistent man who refuses to give up is far removed from what is happening around him. Perhaps he cannot grasp the glaring signals that are being sent to him by the uninterested woman. Or maybe there is an unwillingness to accept the truth that the mind is shouting out so loudly.

A man who insists on pursuing the woman he loves, even when she no longer cares for him, does so because, he somehow believes that his insistence will convince her of the intensity of his love. He thinks that this will cause her to change her mind.

The truth of the matter is that, even if I am loved deeply by someone, the feelings may not be mutual, especially if the thought of marriage is brought up. Be aware that love must be reciprocal if it is to be true and full. One-way love is still love, but, it is not the kind of love that fosters togetherness.

I may love you with all my heart, but if you dislike me, things will not work out for us. I may insist on going on in my one-man campaign to win you over, however, until you return my love with some loving of your own, my efforts will only bring you irritation, and me a lot of frustration.

Remember the song that says: "Please release me. Let me go, for I don't love you anymore." Good advice. The most intelligent thing to do is to recognize that true love does not force itself on an unwilling individual. It must not do violence to the free will of the beloved. If love insists, it will surely cause deep resentment which will take revenge at a later date.

I know many men and women who have allowed the pressure of insistent lovers to get to them. After hesitant marriages, some of these people have somehow come to terms with themselves and are at peace. However, many are very unhappy and now feel terrible regret about having succumbed to the pressure of "insistent" love. Some have reacted and walked away from the relationship. Others continue living in regret, unable or unwilling to break away. They suffer their regret for a number of emotional, religious and social reasons.

Perhaps the best way out of such a situation is the "break." The break is sudden, abrupt and almost always painful. Some try "disengagement" instead because it is less violent and seems to give more time to adjust. I don't agree. I think that "quick is best" more often than not. I agree that it is difficult to cut a relationship suddenly. However, I am completely convinced that it will be a whole lot less painful than presiding over the show and agonizing the death of love.

About the Author

BOB GARON was born in New Hampshire USA. He was sent to the Philippines in 1965 to do missionary work. He left the priesthood and received his dispensation from his vows in 1978. By being involved in organizations that addressed the needs of troubled youth, Bob built a name for himself and is known as the Father of the Therapeutic Community in Asia.

As a writer and columnist, he has written over 14,000 articles over the past four decades. He has helped and inspired countless individuals and couples through his live phone-in counseling on radio and television, as well as with motivational speaking. speaking.

Bob also set-up a management consultancy firm, and, together with his wife Emmy, founded the Golden Values Schools.

Bob now spends his days working with people struggling to overcome various addictions and get their lives back together.

Thank you for reading!

If you received value from this book, please consider leaving a review, however short, on the Amazon page. This will help get the message to others who may need or appreciate it.

Royalties earned from this book will help poor children in the Philippines get an education.

* * *

OTHER BOOKS WRITTEN BY BOB GARON

Loving is Living
Facing Life's Problems
The Challenge of Marriage
Intimate Letters of Married Couples
Intimate Letters of Young Lovers
Reflections on Marriage

Made in the USA
Columbia, SC
26 November 2024